# Cat Book

## Emily Eve Weinstein

*Beau Soleil*
publishing

Library of Congress Catalog Card Number: 2001 095 074

ISBN: 0-9666085-8-5


First Edition, First Printing

Printed in South Korea


Art Photography: Emily Eve Weinstein
Artist Photograph: Anne Bogerd
Editorial Coordination:
John Patrick Grace & Amanda Ballard
Grace Associates, Ltd.
945 4th Avenue Suite 200 A
Huntington, West Virginia 25 701



Beau Soleil Publishing
P.O. Box 23 95
Huntington, West Virginia 25 724

# Contents

# Cat Book
## Introduction

At age three I drew my first cat, Misty. He was a long-haired blue-cream who seized my heart and started me on the path that led to this book. I know first hand how extremely important it is for children to be raised with animals that are treated with love and respect.

Following my rendition of the moon in *Moon Book*, it was time to focus on my other passion, cats. I made a list of 35 people living with approximately 100 cats and then contacted first those who would never speak to me again if their cats weren't included.

Artist Donna Gregory suggested a medium I had never worked with before—monoprints. This medium requires vast patience when you are working with living—and moving!—cats. I ordered a 7"x 9" piece of quarter-inch glass with beveled edges, and then did an oil sketch on the glass. Oh-so-carefully, I centered a piece of paper over the wet oils. By rubbing a wooden spoon in small circles over the paper I then transferred the image. The oil colors had fused but the drawing was still distinct.

Unpredictable as cats themselves, monoprints were the perfect choice, and I began doing the first cats selected for the project.

However, folks phoned to tell of cats like Tubby Nubby weighing 25 pounds; of a couple who made news by being sued for feeding feral cats; of Scarlett, who rescued her five kittens from a Brooklyn building engulfed in flames. The book began to grow.

Yes, every cat has a unique personality—and a story. I am privileged to have been able to paint the cats in this book, and get out their marvelous stories!

v

# Acknowledgments

This project was greatly supported by help from the following: Amanda Ballard, Anne Bogerd, Bonnie Campbell, Jennifer Collins, Patrick Grace, Laura Kagen, Nancy Sears, Jeff Sell, Norman Weinstein and all the cats and their people.

*Dedicated to animal activists everywhere*

*Snappy at Sea*

SNAPPY AT SEA | Snappy and I meet some years ago when I am painting her portrait within a bathroom mural. She keeps me company for hours watching the paint go on the walls of her home. One day she adds her own touch. Snappy walks through my palette of paint and then races down the white carpeted hall leaving a trail of dark green paw prints.

When Snappy's person Pam tells me they are going to sail around the world, I say, "Oh, what a challenge!" (I am of course thinking of Snappy.) Well, the cat has taken to sailing, except when things get rough. Then she glares at Pam, throwing the thought, *Get me out of here, NOW!* At those times Pam wishes she could transport them both instantly to solid ground. But most of the time the sailing is calm, the sun is warm, and Snappy has two people all to herself.

Once, though, she has to fight off an intruder cat that has jumped in from another boat. Snappy has two more years left before she will have sailed around the planet. I catch up with her here in Durham. She and her people have just flown in from LA. Snappy is still fascinated by paint; only now, painting her for the book, I know how closely I must watch her.

**PERSONAL CAT MUSEUM** | At Betsy's personal cat museum, the walls can't be seen because cat imagery from around the world covers every square inch. There is a bronze Egyptian statue two feet tall, an Indonesian cat bench, hand-hooked cat rugs, cat quilts, a highly ornamented cat tree, cat pillows, cat pottery, cat figurines, and of course the extensive cat-book collection.

In 1991, I do a portrait of Roxie, a tortie-point Siamese. I attend Roxie's last birthday party in 1995. She is turning 21 and requires a lot of medical attention. Betsy's philosophy is that the ole gal will be given every chance till her purr and appetite run out. Eventually both do. The vet caring for Roxie phones Betsy at work. She comes and takes the cat home, and Roxie dies in Betsy's arms.

Six months after Roxie's death, Betsy goes to our local animal shelter. A beautiful long-haired white cat purrs up to her and wants to be held. The attendant says, "That's out of character." At her new home, as it turns out, Fermi never allows herself to be picked up again. However, she can be very friendly as she swipes her huge tail over my palette, her white fur becoming every color of the rainbow.

On the day Betsy goes to pick up Fermi, a woman walks in to retrieve a huge Siamese cat with a broad alley-cat body. Frank is stuffed into a very small carrier. Seeing this and the woman's

*Frank, Fermi, and Shirin*

dismay at having to pay the shelter's fee, Betsy offers to take the cat. The woman happily turns him over, not questioning the situation at all and providing no follow-up. As fate has it, Frank gets lucky and so does Betsy. Frank requires no adjustment time; he is just totally happy with every moment of the day. I can't even begin to imagine how anyone could give up such a personable cat.

A year later, a petite long-haired tortie with Persian ancestry joins Betsy's household. Shirin, the namesake of a Persian heroine, has had at least three previous homes. Elderly but feisty, she has made it clear that she would prefer to be the only cat in the house. The other two are simply part of the collection, okay for them to be around, but easy to ignore, as Shirin does with great aplomb.

*Casey in the Sun*

CASEY AND ROMA | While doing the animal shelter mural, I witness people coming in and judging the animals. One of them, a young man, says, "There isn't a dog in here suitable for me." I'm thinking, "You're not even suitable for a stuffed animal!" The worst and the best of humanity walk through a shelter's doors. For instance, the volunteers are living angels. But my paid job here is done, and I need to celebrate by liberating someone. Orange Boy Casey's time is up, and he is doing his best to attract attention, arms stretched out of cage, rubbing and rolling adorably, and purring loudly. In the visitor's room he melts into my arms, requesting never to go back into that cage.

Casey fits in like the missing puzzle piece. My crew and I move to a house on ten acres, and there his personality expands. Casey loves the abandoned barns, the fields, the streams.

4

*Roma Hand Trap*

One day a feral black cat shows up, terrorizing Casey. The stray cannot be caught, nor will he go away. He hisses, growls and behaves dangerously. A friend suggests taming him enough to live-trap and neuter him before releasing him. During the long six months that this plan of action takes place, a fellow New Yorker says, "He's a roma, like me." So he becomes Roma.

The vet, not knowing how to deal with a feral cat, waits three days for his heart rate to go down before she drugs him to work on him safely. Back at the homestead I release the newly neutered cat, saying bye-bye (now go away!). He doesn't. He runs to Casey to hug and kiss him; he rubs the dog down and the outdoor furniture; he kisses the ground; he purrs like a lawn mower. He is *home!* And he wants in.

He loves the house, and I am his person. His second visit to the vet completely astounds the entire staff, as Mr. Terror has become Mr. Love Kitty. Nobody has ever witnessed such a change in an animal. The Casey-Roma connection still has problems. Through animal behaviorists, mediums, behavior modification and herbal remedies, changes are occurring. This morning I see Casey allow Roma to sleep with his paws around him after the morning walk. They've come a long way.

MAIA AND TULI BEAR

Roma is driving me crazy, between spraying the house down, picking fights with Orange Boy Casey, and demanding all my attention. At the end of my tether, I contact animal communicator Tera Thomas. A one-hour consultation leads to better behavior, my approach to the negativity improved, and the herbal remedies Tera prescribed are really working. So, when this *Cat Book* project develops, naturally I ask her for her cat family's story.

Tera feels it is time to get a new companion for her elderly tabby, George. Reviewing a litter of kittens, she is attracted by the pink pads on the three lighter ones, but a darker kitten, with black pads, crawls out to her and Tera places her back. The kitten returns several times before Tera asks, "Are you my kitty?" The kitten rolls over and puts on a show. That night the kitten comes to Tera in a dream and tells her that her name is Maia. When Maia comes home with Tera, she immediately loves the elderly tabby, George, like a big brother. George is not so sure. He has not pictured such a little ball of energy and he does not want to be bothered with her youthful exuberance. But, as Maia grows older, George takes her under his wing and becomes the wise elder.

When tabby George dies, Tera finds herself just as impatient as her clients, wishing for her pet's return via its next incarnation. She asks and the answer comes back the same: "I'll be back." She questions further, "Is there an animal shelter I should go to?" "No, I'll find you." "A pound?" "No, I'll find you." "Respond to an ad?" "No, I'll find you at the right time." So Tera has no choice but to let go and trust that George might or might not come back to her.

Tera's hairdresser complains to her about her cat's new litter in her trailer-salon. Tera asks to see the newborns. Ears still flattened, eyes still closed, a bull's-eye tabby kitten

*Cats with Llamas*

wiggles up into her lap, and once there falls sound asleep.
Tera has a deep knowing of who this little spirit is. When
Tuli-Bear comes home, at first Maia is confused about his
age and size. How can George be this little crazy kitten
who seems so foolish and young? But before long they
renew their bond and now live in harmony with Tera and a
couple of llamas. Neither cat hunts, as the house rule is
that if you're finding your own food, don't expect food
from the human. This and other philosophies have been
imparted through telepathy. Tuli-Bear and Maia are both
teachers at the animal communication workshops where
Tera also teaches. All of the animals that live at
Hummingbird Farm are committed to helping people
deepen their bond with all.

*Natural Allies*

NATURAL ALLIES | Animal communicator Tera Thomas mentions to me that her assistant Jackie has an interesting household. What an understatement! It takes very little enticement to get Dream-Cookie, a thick-coated orange Persian with lion cut, to leap skyward while the black and white rats in their habitat are inspired to climb, mimicking the cat's play. Ferdinand, the three-legged pit-mix dog, is dancing around: "Look at me, I'm pretty cute, too." The delicate Rexes, curled up together under a blanket, are the staid ones as they peer out with wide eyes. Oh,

yes, and across the room in a large cage resides a couple of female brown rats and in a smaller cage, a hamster. This brings the total count to nine in this small duplex.

At age 21, Jackie is told by a friend about a family of unusual cats that have been dropped off at the NYC Humane Society's Shelter after a Devon Rex breeder goes out of business. Jackie adopts a young white male, naming him Plus-One. As a rock-band manager, this means something like "With friends." This sweet ET look-alike is indeed lonely. The shelter having no more Devon Rexes, the young Jackie orders one from a Texas breeder.

The black Rex kitten is just soooo "Hey, Baby" that that is her name: Hey-Baby. The two cats complement each other perfectly. At first shy, once the female Rex gets safe with me, she stretches and rolls over, exposing her near-hairless belly. A more delicate ballerina of a cat I've never met. Then enters the maximum-coated, orange firecracker kitty, Dream-Cookie! Tera, working with Independent Animal Rescue, asks Jackie about fostering this natural clown cat. The "foster" kitty, Hey-Baby finds him to be a great playmate, and Plus-One is shown the proper amount of respect. Jackie sees the cat fit in; the furry wonder is the perfect foil for the near-hairless wonders. When I point out how unusual these cats are, Jackie says, "It's hard for me to have a perspective on what a normal cat looks like."

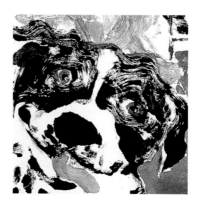

WHISKEY AND BEANER
Dmitri Hammer, a cabinetmaker, says he'd never put up with a cat like my Roma. So here I am at his and his wife's house where not only do the cats have defiant personalities, but also on hand is the blue-eyed, devil dog, Daisy. The other dog they found stumbling along the highway completely blind; her vet bills in the first year were over $2,000. If Dmitri had a cat as demented as Roma, he and Michelle would attempt to solve the problems just as I have. Dang, I well remember Daisy Dog on the job eating everyone's lunch and then heading to the next construction site!

*Whiskey And Beaner*

Anyway, at this house full of animals with exemplary behavior, Michelle comes to the marriage with Whiskey, a sturdy bull's-eye tabby. Michelle's mother does not like cats, so Michelle grows up thinking neither does she. At college she is given the chance to find out differently. As housemates graduate and move on, the cat, Whiskey, gravitates to Michelle. Michelle is flattered and grows into the role of the cat's mom.

In her new home Whiskey misses the company of other cats. So Dmitri hears of an associate's litter and brings home Beaner. Beaner is an unusual athlete. She will climb up high into a tree, but then comes down like a slinky - head first, slink in, spin around, slink down, spin around, head first, slink in, spin around— something that my sensible Roma would never do.

*Mojo Kujo*

MOJO KUJO ELVIS | My dancer friend Molloy is finishing up her teaching degree and working two jobs when a posting at the Durham Public Library for free kittens leads her and her daughter, Jalaika, to an elderly woman with a cat the woman once said "...doesn't need to be spayed because she'll never get out." Well, she does get out on one brief occasion, but that apparently is enough.

The affectionate mother cat, a B&W domestic short hair, has five kittens of various colors. A playful little tabby boy chooses Jalaika, and she dubs him Mojo, which means magic. Mojo seems timid once he is separated from his family and reaches his new home, but that will soon change.

At the time Molloy is rehearsing for a performance with visiting modern dance choreographer Ann Carlson, who is also performing a solo dance depicting the true story of KoKo, the gorilla who learned to communicate through sign language. Ann sends out a call for a kitten. Although Mojo is still getting used to his new environment, Jalaika thinks it will be exciting for him to follow in the family tradition of performing.

Ms. Carlson, completely nude, holds Mr. Mojo in her curled arm or in her mouth like a mother cat as she tumbles, swoops, and swirls, gorilla-like, around the stage. Reportedly Mojo, unlike any previous kitten used in this performance, is completely relaxed and purrs the entire time he is on stage.

Directly after his debut, he is noticeably calmer and more affectionate. He insists on sleeping under the covers with Jalaika and sitting on a lap when anyone sits down. His hair starts to get longer and develop a golden buff undercoat. Mojo now looks like a full-blooded Maine Coon. Who could have known? Once neutered, he settles into his role as man of the house.

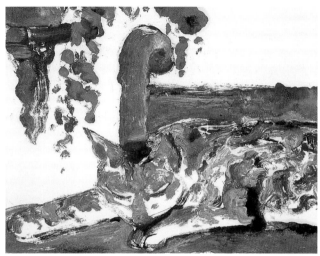

*Copper Pretending to Sleep*

MOTLEY CREW | When I meet Space Cat he is elderly but still very spry, aware, and tremendously affectionate. It is his sweet disposition that has saved his life. Massive amounts of drugs are given to him as a young cat to study the side effects. He is supposed to go deaf, but he doesn't. Having outlived his usefulness at the vivarium, he is slated to be killed, but a student sneaks the sweet cat out the back door of the lab.

Legend has it that the rescued cat is sitting with a bunch of students getting high at "The Ditch," a hippie house down a dirt road by a pond. The cat gazes skyward and his bionic ears begin to twitch. The stoned partiers are convinced he is getting messages from outer space. From then on he is Space Cat, the only permanent resident at The Ditch. For years he lives mainly outside, through snowstorms, heavy rains, unbearable heat. The landlord builds a miniature spiral stair system to the roof for him to escape dogs and receive messages. Kim moves in and, like the other tenants, accepts him as part of the landscape. When she moves out, he sits in the driveway waiting for her return. Her ex-landlord phones saying the cat is depressed. For the first time ever, someone takes sole responsibility for Space Cat, who is much happier in a real home, but then Kim adopts eight-month-old Copper from the Orange County Shelter.

Young calico Copper turns out to be pure alpha temperament. Kim purchases a squirt gun to gain some control. When the plastic object can't be found, Copper does as she pleases. For no apparent reason, except to assure her dominance, she attacks the dog Rasta and the other cat. Not a great hunter herself, Copper steals the victims of other cats and claims them as her own. When wanting canned food, she stares Kim down. "It is like the Exorcist. When this cat's demands are not met she looks possessed."

Kim becomes concerned about the cat's sudden weight gain. Dieting doesn't appear to be helping. Casually talking over the fence to the neighbor, she mentions Copper's mysterious nightly disappearances. It is then she discovers that Ms. Copper, with her evil stare, is demanding food elsewhere. She tells the neighbors to just put her out. "Are you kidding? She would bite me." Evidently Copper's routine next door is dinner, TV and then sleep with the neighbor's husband, or if Kim is lucky Copper comes home.

Exactly six months after burying the 20-to-23-year-old Space Cat under a cherry tree, Kim and I are returning from a hike on the Eno River when a calico kitten approaches. Kim names her Sierra. The dog loves that the new cat isn't mean and occasionally even gets to groom her. Sierra's full, long, silky coat is show-quality in winter, thrift-store reject in summer. She prefers being outside, communing with nature under the cherry tree, avoiding the alpha kitty and Rasta's long and enthusiastic doggy tongue.

**HEALING TOUCH** | At the school where Anita Anglin teaches music, her system is overwhelmed by the toxins released from the fresh paint, the new carpet, and the glue fumes. Chronic fatigue and sinusitis make doing her job impossible, and she is forced to resign. The mainstream doctors she goes to see don't know how to treat her. In Anita's alternative search to deal with her chemical sensitivity, she comes upon the book *The Medical Assistance Program*, by Machelle Wright. It works. It is vibrational healing, and leads to essential Reiki, the art of channeling universal life force energy.

B&W cat Stay-Puft puts his life in danger by eating a long thin palm leaf. Through an expensive medical procedure he is saved. But dang! if he doesn't go and do this again. Same procedure, good outcome, bad bill. Third time Anita decides to put to work what she has learned. The cat is able to relax and vomit up the long strangling leaf.

The voice teacher Anita accompanies on piano notices how her companion dog calms down upon Anita's arrival. She suggests the course Healing Touch for Animals, taught by Carol Komitor. Anita takes to it like she plays piano. "Often when I find an out-of-sync animal, I find a like situation with their human." She finds her companion tortoiseshell Mikey's heart chakra to be out of alignment, like her own.

Mikey's daughter, a 16-year-old tortie point, is withdrawn and quiet. Before her energy training, Anita reads this to be her nature. Her human son Jake, now 23, has been a very high-energy child, being rougher with "his" cat

*Nita's Kids*

Sootie than his brother Andy had been with his Stay-Puft cat. Sootie now hides when Jake returns home. Anita works on releasing her fear and opening her options. Sootie is now sitting close to me purring, watching me paint. When Jake's mother explains the cat's reaction to him, he changes his behavior and now Sootie no longer hides when he visits, but greets him.

"By changing what you say or think about a cat, dog, horse or person, you change the outcome. The cure for my patients includes the whole family." Anita goes over my different energy fields, palms held flat hovering over my body. Fortunately, she has nothing terrible to report, but the rest of the day I feel unusually happy and goofy.

*Murray*

CARACALS | My homeopathic vet, Charles Loops, agrees to adopt two kittens that are slated to be euthanized. Their parents are siblings with a genetic spinal disorder, meaning their offspring will most likely have severe spinal problems. If these young African lynxes are to be adopted out and not destroyed, the new caretakers will have to be prepared to deal with the full ramifications. Dr. Loops is a good candidate, having treated a number of animals at the Florida-based animal preserve. The staff is delighted when he agrees to adopt them. It is heart-wrenching to euthanize any animal, but baby caracals...well, that would be very difficult.

The two taupe and bronze boys, Marley and Murray, have lived their first two years as household pets. They play with the family's dogs and kids. Jeffrey, the thirteen-year-old son, bonds most with them, naturally taking responsibility for their daily care, feeding, changing water, grooming, playing and cleaning up after them (they use the litter box only upon occasion). Marley, his condition being more severe than his brother's, has to have his urine monitored, so with massaging of his bladder he pees into a cup. Doing this twice daily keeps the caracal pee in the house down to one dose. Dr. Loops claims it doesn't have an unpleasant urine odor, but the good doctor also states, "Let's say you want to go into the refrigerator and one of these 35-pound caracals is sitting on top of the fridge, glaring directly into your eyes. You're not going to open the door." At puberty their priorities change, and no matter how much tenderness they are shown early on they revert to their natural ways. Around food they become extremely aggressive.

Now they are living in a 15'x 40' pen. I watch as they nuzzle and groom each other, toss and tumble. I get closer to figure out eye color. Hiss. I sit back down. Hiss. Try to move closer. Hiss. But then Murray rolls over showing a beautiful fleecy white stomach with pale blond dots. I pick up a stick to stroke his magnificent belly. I am told, however, that caracals do know the difference between a stick and flesh. In five years they have not bitten anyone on purpose. This is as tame as caracals get.

REFLECTION | Yoda, a Russian blue, and Tuga, a tortie long hair, live across the street from us. When their person, Maggie, goes out of town, I step in. Tuga greets me, complaining that I'm not there soon enough, quick enough, or long enough. Hissing at me in the beginning, she allows no less than three feet to come between us. Yoda, lounging on either the bed or couch, greets me with an easy smile and purr. Maggie says the two old girls reflect her two sides.

Years ago, following some internal instincts, Maggie lands up in front of the animal shelter. Walking in she is greeted by a tabby named Babe. Babe turns out to be her solace in a destructive marriage. As Maggie untangles the bonds of this poor union, Babe, too, comes out of her shell. When the cat unexpectedly passes to the other side, a

*Tuga, Yoda and Oh Yeah, Maggie*

door opens for Maggie, and she walks out. Maggie grieves the loss of Babe deeply. She knows that Babe has to come back to her. Her son brings her an adorable little barn cat, Tortuga, Turtle in Spanish. Tuga is the name the young tortie prefers. She is not the reincarnation of Babe, however. Maggie continues to look, highly aware of every pet store and animal shelter and occasionally answering ads. No Babe.

Near her home she spots a pet store she has never seen before. Inside, there is just one gray kitten, no other animals. The attendant hands Maggie this only creature. Climbing onto her shoulder, the kitten is clearly saying, "Take me home." After a three-year search, Babe has returned – and into a much better situation. Maggie has remarried a kind, good person named Norm. When asked her name, the new kitten flattens her ears, looking like the Star Wars character Yoda. Her response is identical each time she is asked. So, Yoda she is.

The week after the Yoda adoption, Maggie returns to the pet store for supplies. The store is gone. Sign, cash register, hair balls, all gone. Was it there just as a means for Babe to find her way back?

Both Yoda and Tuga help in Norm's transition as cancer takes him. A decade later Maggie reflects, "We are all getting old together. We all move slower. We are three crotchety old ladies." As I leave, Tuga hisses at me.

*Emma, Kitty and Tiger*

MÉNAGE À TROIS | Sometimes I stop at Julian's after I pick up groceries and film and visit the post office and co-op. On this day he is packing to get out of town with his girlfriend. A pregnant-looking peach tabby shows up. "My sister will be feeding the stray," he says.

I have a better idea. My neighbor Rebecca's cat, named Kitten, is grieving the loss of the other cat. I call her. Bingo! Julian's sister won't have to stop by after all. In fact, the vet already awaits us. Yes, she is pregnant, but healthy. At my neighbor's the cat is instantly at home. She purrs loudly as Rebecca strokes her belly. Daughter Sabrina is thrilled by the thought of kittens. The mourning cat, Kitten, is thrilled, too, but a little scared of his new companion, now dubbed Emma.

Their vet finds Emma's pregnancy odd. She X-rays the pale tabby and sees zip. Sabrina is disappointed. I go back to Julian's neighborhood and find no kittens. Soon after, Emma loses her paunch, gets spayed, fills out all over and falls deeply in love with Kitten.

Happy ending? I think so...until a few months later when I see Rebecca. "I gotta warn you if you

visit. My new housemate has a
cat. Kitten is two-timing
Emma." I am devastated for
the poor stray that I'd found a
good home for. Kitten visits,
grooms, cuddles, sleeps with
the other cat, and then returns
to Emma. Disgusting!

   Not more than a week later Rebecca calls me. "Don't
worry; they are now a happy unit of three. Emma and the
new cat, Tiger, are forging a friendship, and Kitten is
certainly no longer lonely." How could I forget that three
is an extremely strong number for cats?

*Third Party*

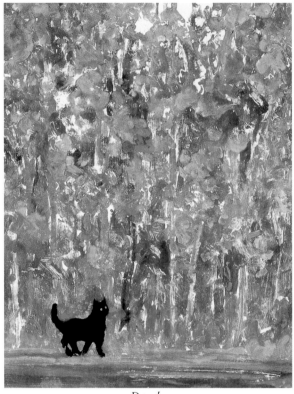

*Dazzle*

DAZZLE | Living temporarily in Upstate New York as Michael does his internship, Wendy decides it is time to add a cat to their family. With Caleb, four, and Eliza, only two, they go to the local shelter. There they find a litter of three kittens that look totally unrelated. Caleb chooses the blue-cream tabby, while Eliza seems to be attracted to the tortoiseshell, and Mom Wendy, falling for the black one, says, "Oh, Daddy needs a kitten too!" The shelter allows the family to adopt all three. "With a toddler? Did they know the kids' ages?" "Yes, we all went."

In Dazzle's first year, young Eliza accidentally slams his tail in a door. With children in pajamas, Wendy rushes the cat to the emergency clinic where two inches of limp tail are amputated. They move back to Durham where Dumbo, the blue- cream, is hit by a car. Barney, a very friendly tortie wanders away and, in spite of flyers, news-paper ads, the works, is never found. Only introverted Dazzle remains. "With young children it is impossible to restrict where an animal goes. Dazzle's cautious nature saved him."

Here in Durham, now with three children, Wendy and Michael build a large sherbet-colored house near the woods and me. Dazzle now enjoys a very safe existence. Wendy tells me the cat is mostly bonded to her. Eliza states, "I feed him and give him the most attention." Caleb yells, "No you don't! He sleeps on my feet at night, and I feed him." Four-year-old Zach screams, "NO! I feed him!" When Dr. Michael comes home, he says to me, "How nice, you're including my cat." Wendy explains the cat makes the rounds but at present is nowhere in sight. I've only seen him from afar and might never get to paint him up close. Oh, well.

*Mercedes*

MERCEDES | On a visit to my folks in NYC I ask if they know of any city cats. Mom immediately thinks of her former co-worker Marilyn who had been deathly afraid of cats, but now lives with one.

Marilyn recounts that as a very young girl in the Bronx, she had a large black cat come through her bedroom window like a possessed demon in the dead of the night and land on her bed with a tremendous thud. She wakes the household with her scream. Marilyn's father is annoyed. Simply a cat? To Marilyn it is not a cat, but a monster.

From that day on she avoids cats, crossing the street if she sees one, asking people to lock the family pet safely away from her. She does, however, love dogs. In fact, when her dog Chloe dies, Marilyn volunteers with an AIDS organization to walk the canines of AIDS patients. Another Marilyn in the building sees that she is a kind person who can be counted on, so she approaches her about a cat that needs a home. The first Marilyn tells her about her phobic past. In the meantime a neighbor's shy cat daily investigates the hallway and stairs. He runs when he sees Phobic Marilyn. This daily, non-threatening encounter is gently

*Mercedes in Pink Chair*

wearing her fear down.

Meanwhile, City Critter volunteer Marilyn II rescues her first cat off the streets of Bedford Stuyvesant and is desperate to place her. She asks Marilyn I again and again until the latter relents. At this time the rescued stray is used to a life of spotty meals, heavy traffic, constant noise and filth. A home away from the chaos would be heaven. For the first night Marilyn leaves all the lights on so her eyes will not be scratched out.

In the morning she still has both her eyes—and the cat Mercedes is in the same spot, still asleep. All is as it was the night before. They have since developed their symbiotic routines, and Marilyn now believes she will never again be without a cat.

CITY CRITTERS |  Marilyn is most insistent that I meet another Marilyn, a retired school teacher and one of the founders of City Critters. Muffin, a pastel calico, comes out to greet me. I sit down and Muffin is in my lap. Other cats scatter. "Marilyn, this is the perfect cat." "She is a thief, she steals Ramona's special dietary food. And besides, she will have nothing to do with the others."

A large tortie is staring at me malevolently. "Peanut is my problem cat. Don't go near her. She loves only me." I remember the other Marilyn saying she couldn't come in here because of an aggressive cat. Peanut approaches me, I offer my hand, she smells it. Marilyn II holds her breath. "Oh good, you didn't get bit. Don't push your luck." Phone rings again and someone yells, "Marilyn, I know you're there. Pick up." She does, more debates on a poten- tial adopter. I go to wash out a brush and a long high yowl- ing growl comes from Peanut. She is blocking the door. Marilyn stands between us so I can use the sink. Peanut likes only Marilyn. She is blocking the door again and dares me to pass her. I do, gingerly, as she attacks my blue jeans, making an ancient warrior's cry.

"We don't only place cats and the occasional dog." One time Marilyn gets looped into carting two full-grown Easter chicks found in the projects out to a farm on Long Island. Sent with her is the dreary teenage son of the woman who found the chickens. The young man's role is to carry the small cat carrier these two birds are squeezed into. He neither talks to nor acknowledges Marilyn the entire five hours. Between hot train ride, miserable boy, and pecking hens in plastic carrier, Marilyn paints a picture of hell. Back in the city she buys her traveling companion dinner. He orders chicken. In her studio apartment she crashes onto her bed, pressing play on the answering machine...

Fellow City Critter volunteer Naomi yells, "Help! I just went to a French restaurant and rescued twelve frogs. I don't know how to deal with frogs. They are leaping all over my bathroom! You must come and help me."

*Muffin, the Perfect Cat*

Marilyn, absolutely exhausted but knowing her partner is a very serious person, knows this is a very real dilemma. She phones Mary, the one who got her to take zombie boy with chickens out to Long Island. She leaves a message passing on Naomi's need for help and then phones Naomi. Naomi says incredulously, "You believed me?" "Yes." "Because you don't have a sense of humor, and this proves it!"

"But this is what makes it all worthwhile." Marilyn brings out a thank-you letter accompanying a beautiful photograph of two full-grown cats embracing and smiling into the camera. A stray has been placed with a lonely apartment cat, and here they are two weeks later completely bonded. "This is what my work is all about and why I wake up each day and continue with it."

*Taormina*

TAORMINA | Heading uptown with City Critter flyers, I feel possessed to help Marilyn in her never-ending mission. My next stop is my neighbor Wendy's younger sister Ellen, who lives here in NYC on the Upper East Side. She introduces me to the very beautiful Taormina, another North Shore Animal League success story. I say, "How sad that she is all alone." "You think so?" "Absolutely." "You don't think she is too old to introduce another cat?" "Absolutely not!" Ellen works full-time at Mt. Sinai Hospital as a clinical-care social worker, evenings she sees her own clients, and she attends New York University as a Ph.D. candidate; also, the phone never stops ringing.

Ellen has a dream about getting a kitten. "Wouldn't it be more work?" "Less, because the cats would occupy each other." "How would I introduce them?" "Marilyn would set everything up. You would have excellent help every step of the way." She agrees to phone Marilyn in two weeks. The answering machine takes all the calls. I don't think anyone in NYC answers her phone directly anymore.

Taormina is at first shy. She is a true tri-colored tabby with orange rust bands between darker bands. She has the perfect heart-shaped face with lime-green eyes. Ellen brings work home in order to share as much quality time with Taormina as possible. She regrets listening to the first vet's insistence on declawing. He explained, "She will ruin your furniture; she doesn't need them at all." Ellen explains to me the things Taormina can't do, having had this operation. I get paint on the off-white couch and it turns out that she doesn't care about the furniture. I get the paint off, but now the watermark left behind is the size of a small ugly lake. Ellen casually turns the pillow over. She has a paper to write and two meetings this evening, and the phone rings every thirty seconds. No wonder no one answers the phone around here.

Taormina stares at me. She is interested in the treats I've brought, but mainly for the new smell. She gets a whiff of something she doesn't like and hisses at me. Probably Marilyn's aggressive Peanut has left a nasty message on my supplies, and Taormina has read it. Ellen apologizes for pushing me out, but in truth she is remarkably polite as I've stayed two hours over after arriving an hour late and ruined a cushion on her couch. I hope she phones Marilyn.

*Kitty*

## MOHAMMED LEAVES, KITTY ENTERS

Next, I go downtown to the East Village where Ellen and
Wendy's brother Andrew lives with his partner, Shaffiq,
from Kenya, and a very green eyed, bull's-eye tabby, Kitty.

Fifteen years old, Mohammed, a mackerel tabby, has
always wandered out into the hall and come back. No
problem. One day she doesn't. Within an hour of her
disappearance Andrew has plastered the neighborhood
with posters stating the mildly senile cat needs insulin.
"Please help me find her!" Calls come in almost immediately; she has been sighted, but no one has picked up the
slow-moving cat. Andrew calls the Center for Animal
Control and Care. They claim not to have a sick elderly
tabby. A phone call comes in from directly behind their
building. Andrew goes straight over. A man holds out a
young glossy-coated bull's-eye tabby with bright green
eyes. "I found it, please take it, I can't deal with it." The

guy puts the cat down outside, walks away, and closes his door. The young beauty bolts across the street, nearly getting hit. Andrew catches up to her, she purrs, rolls over, and offers her fleecy belly with dark contrasting spots. What is Andrew to do? You guessed it. She settles into her new digs immediately. Calls keep coming in.

A woman phones. She has taken Mohammed to the Center for Animal Control and Care and given Andrew the case number. He is told he will have to come in. "Tell me over the phone, do you have her or what?" "You have to come in." Andrew goes to the place with a sinking feeling. They have put her down sooner than the 24-hour minimum permitted for sick cats. They are better known for control than care. Sixty thousand animals are euthanized here every year. Bottom line, millions live in this city and thousands lose or abandon their pets; the place is overwhelmed. It is best to visit animal facilities in person immediately, and often, make yourself known, make the staff aware of you and the lost one. (Please see "Lost and Found," fifth paragraph.)

An elderly woman that speaks only Polish feeds hundreds of pigeons a day in the back and front of the brownstone. The pigeons demolish Andrew's garden. Kitty, through the kitchen window, goes out along the high brick wall surrounding the small courtyard to get close to the squirrels. She runs in when the pigeons cover the entire walled-in "garden" with flapping wings. After they leave, the Polish woman scrubs up their mess. She is kind to Kitty, and Kitty enjoys the daily show this generous pigeon feeder/garden killer provides.

Andrew tells me, "Kitty is the sweetest cat. She never complains about a thing." Of course, given this deluxe kitty condo with its free daily bird show versus a short, hard life on the mean streets of NYC, what's to complain about? Andrew heads off to work at *The New York Times*. Shaffiq is just getting up. He is a doctor working crazy hours. In these chaotic households where people live busy lives, cats play a most important role. They soothe the nerves and offer meditative moments of unconditional love and support, so doctors can save lives and writers can inform the world.

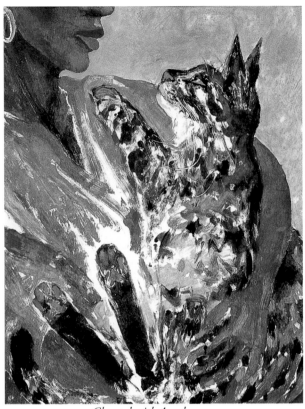

*Chrystal with Angel*

TWINS AND FANGS | At the Edible Art Auction, fellow New Yorker Chrystal Austin tells me, "I'll have to see this next book of yours as half my family is cat, you know." It seems that Chrystal's twin boys, Jordan and Ari, and daughter, Nasia, feel that 16-year-old tabby Diamond is attached only to their mother. The ten-year-old boys and budding teen want cats that relate to them personally.

At the Orange County Animal Shelter, the twins pick out solid black twin boys. Nasia chooses a healthy-looking gray kitten, but when the shelter workers look up her paper work they discover she is already spoken for. The sickly little runt in the same cage is available, but otherwise is going to be euthanized shortly. Nasia opts for the scrawny tabby. "I stayed out of the decision making," Chrystal says. "I didn't want to influence their choices, but remarkably they chose cats that have grown to resemble

*Giant Twins*

their personalities."

The runt, Angel, grows to a normal size and has an affectionate, calm personality like Nasia. The twins, both human and feline, are playful, curious and rambunctious. But these cats have some unusual things about them. They are presently only thirteen months old, and already Blacky and Fiesty are 16 pounds each without being fat. Their heads and paws are huge, and their limbs are long. Could their mother have mated with some kind of large, exotic cat? The enormous adolescent cats are sprawled out on the upper level of kitchen cabinets looking down. Their size makes it a scene out of the Twilight Zone.

Not to be overshadowed, Angel has a remarkable feature, too. She has eight fangs. Normally, at four-six months the adult teeth push the baby teeth out, but in truth this looks like eight adult fangs. Totally bizarre. Tabby Angel will play with only one giant cat at a time and retreats when both are present. Feisty is gnawing on my supplies; Blacky has just landed in a flying leap into my paint box - THUD! I haul them off my supplies and realize that the 16-pound estimation of their weight feels more like 30. I need to return in a few months to see if Angel is still eight-fanged and how much larger these adolescent giants have gotten.

*Sudi with Birds*

MUSICAL ANIMALS | Since I've known Cindy and Francis Vega, there has always been an animal saga going on at their place. We first meet when I am commissioned to do a mural of their blacksmithing operations. One of the shop's dogs sits centrally in the image. At their large home there are three sets of animals that never meet.

The female cats Sudi and, until she dies, Roxy, get along peacefully; they have the run of the house, sleeping upstairs in the huge bedroom with Cindy, Francis and the six birds. Harry and Willie, a couple of burly brown tabbies, occupy the basement apartment until Estrella Vega, Francis's mother, moves in with Valentina, a chow-mix. This is when the game of "Musical Animals" begins.

When Valentina is sleeping in her room or out with her person, and Sudi is sequestered in the bird bedroom, Harry and Willie are let out to play about the house. When Harry and Willie are in their room and Valentina is closed up or out of the house, it's Sudi's turn to be free. Three sets of animals that don't ever get the chance to meet, and with good reason.

Cindy finds a tiny, hungry soot-covered kitten trapped in the bowels of a piece of machinery at their blacksmith shop. A week later at their new home the Vegas proudly introduce me to the newest member of their family, the scrawny Sudi bolting all over the massive house.

Then come The Boys. Neighbors call. Four or five cats are wandering aimlessly on the road. All of them are about eight months old, appear healthy and clean, but are traumatized to varying degrees. One of the cats is easily caught and goes on to a good home. Francis and Cindy end up with the most traumatized. It takes several days for Francis to coax two other cats out of the woods and towards the house. Harry is finally caught and safely installed in the basement. Willie is still out there for another week, cold, hungry, scared, and confused. Cindy scours the landscape daily for the cats. While sitting on the front porch during a rain storm, she hears a rustle beside her; huddled in a plant is one of the cats, now known as Willie. She snatches him up in a towel and manages to get the kicking and screaming lad to the basement with his brother. They never are able to find the other orphans. Evidently, bad people were depending on good people to take in this crew.

Harry and Willie prove to be aggressive towards Sudi and Roxy. Cindy gets fed up with their actions and puts them out the front door. They never move from the place, but just sit staring through the door window, trembling. She finally gives in and lets them back inside.

The chow, Valentina, proves to be aggressive towards cats, so the Boys get the other upstairs bedroom, two large windows with expanded sills, three scratching posts and a double bed. Because all the cats are kept in safety zones, they are shy of strangers. Sudi, no longer scrawny, is known as "the keeper of the birds." She sits very pleasantly with us. The birds are another story, squawking and chirping, "Look at us, look over here, pay attention to us!" So, as can be seen by this monoprint, I do.

It's musical animals at the Vega's.

*Tubby, Mikey and Jake*

LOST AND FOUND | After finishing the mono-
print at the Vega's, Cindy insists I meet Jammin Jake, the
brother of their boys, Harry and Willie. I am in a rush but
agree to dash over with her. Glad I did! Three amazing cat
tales in one place.

Ellyn and Tom Fourqurean are returning home from
the movies when, as they are coming around the corner
onto their road, their headlights reflect off many cat eyes.
It appears that an entire litter of adolescent cats has been
dumped. They phone their neighbors, Francis and Cindy,
who join them in pajamas. Without much difficulty Tom
catches a black-and-white cat and places him inside his
coat on top of his belly. The cat nestles in, becoming "Jake
and the Fat Man."

Unfortunately, Jake bites Ellyn during the rescue. He is

quarantined at the shelter, but Tom pays the 80 bucks and after two weeks Jake comes home. The robust Jake, being the least traumatized, I find to be completely socialized, unlike Willie and Harry. There is still a sibling that no one has been able to catch, but over the past three years there have been sightings.

Back in 1989, prior to Jammin Jake's arrival, Mikey, a neighbor's cat, adopts Tom and Ellyn's home as his. They move and Mikey goes with them with the approval of his original family. Going for a week's vacation to Hilton Head, the couple board both Mikey and their ancient cat, Miss Priss, for the first time at a kennel. Returning from their trip, they go straight to the kennel. The attendant looks distraught and gets someone from the back to break the news. They have lost Mikey. No explanation. Ellyn and Tom insist on searching the kennel top to bottom.

With the help of friends and Mikey's former family, they search throughout Chapel Hill. On a rainy thundering night, Ed and Cindy Geiger, their friends, go out with them and get drenched. Ellyn says, "Every phone post had a flyer, I knocked at every door in Chapel Hill, and I checked the shelter every day it was open." The out-of-state owner of the kennel flies in to deal with the Fourqurean's lawyer. For three months Mikey's people feel constant despair, and then a phone call comes. An employee from the Orange County Animal Shelter, well acquainted with the story, is out  walking his dog when he thinks he may have seen The Cat. At his house he phones Ellyn. It takes a week of combing the area before Mikey is finally found. He has lost half of his 14 pounds, his small upper and lower teeth are gone, and he can scarcely meow. At the clinic his purr is so loud that the vet cannot check his heart. She snaps her fingers, makes loud noises, dips his paw in water. Mikey simply will not stop purring!

*Tubby Nubby*

During Ellyn's frequent trips to the shelter, searching for Mikey, she meets a mother bobtail and her newborns that have been dropped off by their "owner." When they are weaned she brings a highly sociable sweet little bobtail kitten home. Tubby, by all accounts, is just a happy, laid-back, funny little cat that wags her little nubby tail when asked a question. Very cute...but around her second year she starts getting big.

The vet says, "No concern, she's a happy, healthy, active cat." She continues to expand. She enjoys sitting upright with belly exposed, attracting lots of attention, as people marvel at her size. When she tops out at 25 pounds, she is placed on a permanent diet. Amazingly, Tubby Nubby can stand up on her hind quarters for dietary treats, just as her normal sized companions, Jammin Jake and Mikey, do.

GOLDEN BOY'S MOM |  Painting Duke Chapel under a full moon, I notice cats living in the shadows of the Gothic church. Later I hear about Helen Cook, a Duke nurse, who has attacked the feral-cat problem humanely and has influenced others to help. Here I am at her condominium. As we sit and talk, I am holding an adolescent cat that had been reverting. "Tori is a true feral that likes to influence others, so cats that can revert I separate from her. Having a safe stranger hold Thea helps socialize her." Large Golden Boy flops onto his mom, letting me know he owns Helen. Born feral, he is now very distant from that original ginger tabby.

"I love dogs as much as cats but they don't work with my crazy schedule." At present Helen has been up 30 hours, testimony to the nursing shortage in hospitals. "The general public doesn't have a clue as to what we do. I extrapolate much from my nursing to help the cats." Now the main volunteer anesthetist for the Raleigh chapter of Operation Catnip, she describes how a shelter has instructed her to trap some feral kittens so they could be socialized and adopted out. However, once the kittens are brought in they are euthanized. "This is my introduction to feral cats and it impacts me greatly. There is no place for them."

Two years later Helen finds a feral colony at Duke's Credit Union by following a sickly kitten to his litter. As she is temporarily leaving town, she calls on fellow nurse and friend Beth to help with the situation. After two hours Beth catches him, but the vet says he is probably too sick to make it. However, Beth toils to save the young life, and succeeds, naming him Wheatie. But Helen and Beth know that the problem extends well beyond this one cat. Not wanting to chance another miscommunication with a shelter, Helen purchases three safe traps and captures three

*Golden Boy and Bessie*

feral cats. The kittens are also caught, then socialized and placed as pets. As the three crated feral cats get used to Beth's basement, Helen and Beth get accustomed to them and think about their next step.

Remarkably the cover story for Zoophile, a free animal newspaper, describes the fledgling group Operation Catnip, dedicated to TNR (trapping, neutering, releasing). The to-be founder Julie Levy agrees to inoculate and alter all three for $15.00 each, but now what to do with the unadoptable group? When asked if the newly altered cats could be returned to where they were found, the president of Duke's Credit Union says, "Who am I to say otherwise? This is their home." It takes four years thereafter of consistent TNR before there are no more kittens in this location, but those subsequent litters are robust because of good nutrition.

A Duke student contacts them about another colony near Duke Chapel. With Elizabeth Balogh, they discover clusters of mothers with kittens. "Elizabeth writes the president of Duke University asking for their blessings to continue with what we are doing. We are called in for a meeting with Jack Burgess, the Director of Facilities Management. By this time the feral cat population is huge. Jack is not only cordial, but also offers resources." What this has translated into is safe traps, an account with Operation Catnip, and help to TNR administrator Helen from the Facilities Management supervisor, David Atwater.

After an article in the *Duke Dialogue* about feral and abandoned cats, other people begin to maintain feral cat colonies. All the cats at the colonies Helen looks after have names. At Duke Chapel, the names are biblical; at the Credit Union, there are Credit and Debit. As Helen says, "Every kitty deserves a name and a home, but not every home deserves a kitty."

*Sandra's Cat Family*

FOREVER | Laura's eyes water and she sniffles when she enters my home, but despite my friend's sensitivity she is remarkably connected to cat people. Through Laura I meet Sandra, who, as a young adult, has picked up her first kitten, Chachi, at the local flea market. At the vet's she learns about ingrown-collar syndrome. Simply put, the kitten's original family, besides not being too bright about neutering and spaying, also did not know about loosening an animal's collar as it grew. Sandra, knowing nothing at this time about cats and wanting to be an excellent cat owner, buys the entire new-pet package: spaying, microchipping, tattooing, and declawing.

Young Sandra, realizing there is a lot to having a cat, gets hired at a veterinarian clinic. Through Harley, cat two, she witnesses it all. No sane person will argue the point of spaying/neutering, and anyone that has had a beloved pet returned because of microchip and tattoo identifiers will declare them necessities. But declawing? She is horrified. The last joint is

clipped off – blood everywhere, paws forever shortened, making the cat an amputee. Now she understands why Chachi cried for two solid days and nights, and now poor Harley is undergoing the same torture. Sandra will never help declaw another cat and has since talked many out of it. In truth, I have never understood doing this to cats. My folks' business involves antique wood furniture, highly desirable for scratching. A section of a wall is carpeted just for the cats. Both the furniture and the cats stay blissfully intact.

Of course, over time other cats came to Sandra. A little girl brings in a stray kitten, which has almost been eaten by her Rottweiler, only eventually to become Ju-Bei, 16 pounds with claws. Willow is also chosen for the Sandra clan, and there is a completely feral cat named Tristan. I am struck by the calmness of this multi-cat household; in the four hours I am there, no territory fights occur. Sandra explains, "Cats need each other; they are inter-bonded. Cats are highly sociable. Cats take care of each other, but some need more territory. Those kind don't choose to be

here. Anyway, what makes them particularly secure is knowing that not only am I dedicated to them their entire lives, but they are also dedicated to me for mine." With that she turns around and exposes her back. There, tattooed in a hipster belt imbedded in her skin forever, is each of her four-legged family members beautifully represented in full color.

*Chico's Tummy*

HUNTER AND CHICO | Laura goes with me to Winston-Salem to pack up an exhibit. Afterwards we fall in with a bunch of people I'd never met before, so I ask my question, "Does anyone have an amazing cat story?" Tom, a writer, answers the quickest, "Yes, my cat Chico!"

Tom's brother, Hunter, dies in 1996 as a result of highly toxic drugs prescribed to him because he has tested positive for HIV antibodies four years earlier. Tom's subsequent reading about HIV and the history of its discovery leads him to question mainstream medical views on AIDS and its treatment, and to conclude that the drugs prescribed to Hunter were unnecessary and have been the sole cause of his death. A brilliant writer, environmentalist and animal communicator dead at the age of 41.

On the eve of the fourth anniversary of Hunter's passing, at the stroke of midnight, Tom

*Chico in the Tub*

is raging, fuming, feeling every bit of that initial hurt, grief, anger. When Dora, his wife, reminds him that the kids are sleeping, he storms out onto the front porch and is stopped in his tracks by a kitten he has never seen before. The little animal trots up the steps, pauses, and then leaps into Tom's arms, purring as though he has always known him. The despair and darkness are replaced instantaneously by the joy and love of this small animal. Chico reminds Tom of what Hunter had been all about.

*In the Backyard*

CAT FAMILY | I'm always impressed with people that have been raised anti-cat but break through and find the cat lover within. Jan spots a litter of Maine Coons on a trip up to Quebec City. It is instant love, but between travel and a lingering uncertainty, she does not move on her desire. Back in the US, moving into a friend's old place, Jan announces, "I'm going to get a cat." The friend says, "Well, congratulations. A feral one comes with the place." Jan never sees the creature until, a few weeks later, there, in the crotch of a tree, a cat sits watching her. Her long fur matches the color of the bark. Has she been watching all this time? Only now revealing her presence? She deems Jan okay and accepts the invitation to make the indoor transition and to be dubbed Oo-tay.

The vet believes Oo-tay may have already been spayed, pointing to something that may have been a scar, but then again, he feels she might already be pregnant. Indeed, in her present lifestyle she is filling out. Her brown tabby coat is getting long and shiny, and she is looking like a large version of the beautiful litter Jan saw in Quebec.

On Christmas Eve, a scrawny white cat appears in Jan's picture window. She has to leave for dinner with her folks. Jan decides she will deal with the stray cat when she gets back, hoping he will not be there. He is gone—but periodically she does see him. A weather advisory states that all pets should come in from the outside. He shows up and is indeed delighted to come in. In fact, when Jan picks him up, the to - be White E. Boy places arms around Jan's neck and nuzzles his big head against her, emitting a feeling of thank you, thank you, thank you. His hard days are over.

Valentine's Day weekend comes and the two best friends, Oo-tay and White E. Boy, disappear. Jan is desperate. When they show up Monday, Jan swoops her cat-kids up and off to the vets. White E. Boy has to get neutered and Oo-tay, well, she may or may not be pregnant. Jan is sick of this. Either she is or she isn't! An X-ray reveals one tiny kitten spine. Jan opts not to abort and spay, but holds off travel or any extensive plans to await the magic moment. A box with padding is placed in a quiet, safe closet. Oo-tay comes to her with her stomach contorting. They go to the box and Oo-tay jumps in and delivers a little tortie-cream; then a long time after that a large, talkative kitten; and finally the last, a black-and-white boy Jan has to help with.

Oo-tay proves to be a perfunctory mother, jumping out when she has finished the basics. Then White E. Boy jumps in to groom, nuzzle, play and sleep curled around his kittens.

Someone at work mentions wanting a black and white one, and others might have been interested, but Jan keeps off the subject. Give away her family? Which one? How horrible. About the time the young cats are neutered/spayed, Jan's mother stops asking when they will be placed. A decade later a family of five cats, all over twelve pounds, know where they've come from and where they're staying.

*YumYum*

**YUMYUM AND KOKO** | Gail answers an ad: "New owner allergic, beautiful lynx-point Siamese sisters." Despite the description hardly fitting the outdoor tabbies before her, Gail adopts YumYum & KoKo on the spot. At their new home she is surprised at how easily they adapt to being indoor cats. She is concerned, however, over their dislike of the cheap food she was given by the previous "owner," Olivia. She phones Olivia requesting the real previous owner's number. Olivia refuses to give it. "She's in a nursing home, you mustn't bother her." Okay, she has relatives, friends? Gail insists on a contact number for these cats. Finally the ex- "new owner" relinquishes the name and number of the previous owner's sister, Della, in Richmond, Virginia.

Della is stunned to learn that YumYum and KoKo, the beloved companions of her sister, Martha, have been given away. Miss Martha is almost impossible to convince to make the move to the Richmond nursing home. She does not want to leave the cats, but she can no longer care for them. She doesn't have a choice. The real estate agent finds a cat-friendly buyer that will maintain the cats in the manner to which they are accustomed. That said, the buyer is given a substantial discount on the house; the buyer of course being the woman Gail got the free "lynx-point Siamese" from.

Basically, the day the allegedly cat-friendly home buyer moves in is the last day these ten-year-old indoor cats see the inside of their home. Olivia disregards the agreement that had landed her the cats' home, well below market value. The health food runs out, and cat-friendly home buyer Olivia buys junk they are unaccustomed to. Gail's investigations do not stop. At KoKo and YumYum's original vicinity, neighbors tell her of YumYum being chased up a tree by a dog; when, after a week, the "new owner" does nothing, the neighborhood mobilizes and hires a service to get the cat down.

Until Miss Martha passes away, Gail writes her weekly letters from her beloved YumYum and KoKo. KoKo has since joined Miss Martha on the other side, but the cat's original pet sitter, Miss Violet, still visits YumYum monthly.

*With Neighbor*

AND NEIGHBOR MAKES THREE | George answers my ad looking for a pet sitter. During the ten days I am gone he takes my instructions regarding Roma seriously. I ask the new pet sitter to give the ex-feral cat lots of attention so he won't revert. George moves his work onto my computer, in essence moving his office here so the cats and dog will have a full-time person. He works with Roma in his lap, carries him around and manages to give the others plenty of attention too. As a lonely bachelor, George is a great pet sitter. When he meets his new girlfriend and future wife Ann, with her cats Figgy and Maxine, his life becomes full and we lose a dedicated sitter. Tabby Figgy bonds tightly with his human dad. His sister Maxine becomes warmer and bonds with her human mom. They sleep on the side of the bed with their preferred parent.

Eleven years ago, Ann mentions to a friend that works in another department in her environmental consulting firm that she wants to get a kitten. The friend agrees to pass on the word to someone in the department named Catherine whose cats had kittens. Ann phones when the cats are already weaned. "Yes, I kept out a kitten for you, but when I find the other one Momma Kitty hid from me, I'll be gassing that one." Ann is stunned, but quickly says, "No, I'll take that one, too." Turns out the cat has had eleven kittens. The fellow employee has taken ether home from work, placed the kittens in a plastic bag and has killed nine. The mother cat, realizing something terrible is up, manages to save one. Ann offers to get the mother cat spayed. Catherine refuses, saying she doesn't have the time. Shortly thereafter she moves from the area with the cat and her daughter.

The two surviving kittens, Maxine and Figgy, grow big and strong and have excellent medical care, unlike their poor mother. They live off a gravel road in a quiet neighborhood in a big house with a cat door opening onto their deck and large garden. As I come up to their house, a very cross-eyed Himalayan snowshoe greets me. "And who is this?" Turns out the neighbor's Little Bit is super-gregarious and must have company all the time. Figgy likes him, but Maxine finds his presence irritating. "Odie," as Ann and George have renamed him, is an excellent diplomat and gives the irritable Maxi her space. He is now sprawled out in their kitchen. Maxi is muttering some curses at him.

Odie-Little Bit's people come home. I go over to get the rest of the cat's story. They wish he'd stay home more. I mention his need for companionship, and they are certainly not adverse to getting a second cat at a less hectic time. Meanwhile, he is now sprawled out in his other  kitchen, equally at home in both places.

*St. Francis with the Cats*

ROAD KILL | Jennifer, who herself has rescued
scores of cats and kept six, tells me of a cat she will never
know, hit by a car and left lying out at a busy intersection
in full view. She passes this freshly killed cat one day as
she drives to work. Jennifer feels her usual mortification
that the motorist did not stop. Perhaps the cat had a
chance. Not anymore. The next day the corpse is still
there. And the next day
and the next. The
deceased feline is
rained on, dried
out, and continues
to be one with the
daily sites. No one
has stopped to show

this once-living creature enough respect to remove it from the road.

After a week of this, Jennifer and her husband Jeff go to fetch the body for a proper burial. The cat's body is gone. Jennifer is in action mode; she wants to do something in memory of the cat's life and untimely death. She orders a huge deluxe wreath of flowers for the unknown road victim. She does so even while telling herself none of the human drones in cars will know or care.

The magnificent wreath is placed at the site. A few days later she sees votive candles at the cat's shrine. In days following more tokens are left. Jennifer's heart lifts, but it is the day when she sees the store-bought card of a cat placed amongst the offerings that she knows others have felt and understood the value of this solitary feline life.

*Peaceable Kingdom*

PEACEABLE KINGDOM | In a homey bungalow my friend Kitty has created a warm and secure world with three dogs, three cats, a turtle, and five fish. She herself did not grow up in anything remotely like this. Her mother died when she was eight and by 14 what negligible support she had had vanished. She got herself to school and clothed and fed herself and took menial jobs. Now, almost thirty years later, working as a fire inspector, attending school by night, writing in the wee hours, gardening on weekends, Kitty has a full life.

She has been frustrated, however, by not being able to write full-time. She is thinking/feeling those very thoughts when she hears a faint mew at her front door. It is a tabby-

Abyssinian kitten on a bitter-cold night beseeching Kitty to let her in. Kitty picks up the tawny boy and asks, "Are you my Muse?" He purrs, "Yes." The lithe Muse is readily accepted by mellow Milo and sweet tabby Abigail, and the dogs know basically how to ignore cats. Emily, a corgi mix, is the only one that will tell a cat off with a quick bark.

For her birthday, 14 years ago, her sister gives her Abigail. For her 38th birthday, Kitty decides she needs some male energy in the house, so at the pound she chooses full-grown, orange and white Milo. The gentle giant turns out to be a perfect fit. Now Turtle Frankenbeetle is meandering around. He is fairly inquisitive toward the new person in the house. Kitty shows me a horrible photo of his shell split in pieces, guts exposed, legs splayed out. This was once Frankenbeetle. He was rushed by Kitty to turtle expert Jim Lee, who placed his entrails back in the correct locations, bonded the shell together with wire and designed and fitted fiberglass scales. Frankenbeetle is now happily one of the clan. In summer he goes to an outdoor enclosure.

The cats get to go out when Kitty is home. She takes an empty gallon plastic jug and attaches it to a six-foot leash connected to the collar. This seems to allow for  mobility but prevents scaling of the high wooden fence and killing of small beasts. "It's amazing how peaceful your animals are together." Kitty says, "It's the one law."

*Nellie and Panda*

SISTERS | Sophie has died, and now Hal and Anne are discussing one cat versus two cats in light of the present void. At the shelter two black-and-white kittens, same coloring as their beloved Sophie, stretch their paws out to them. The two tumble about their cage together, stopping to groom each other. The one versus two debate is answered.

Their kids name the sisters Panda and Nellie. At 8 p.m. each evening all the children, Emma, Jake, Nellie and Panda, pile onto a bed for the bedtime story. When it is finished Emma peeks under the covers and asks, "Did you two like that one?"

*Walter and Ruby*

WALTER AND RUBY | Ruth is working as a cook in Franklin, North Carolina, for Outward Bound when someone in the group finds a litter of kittens by the side of a road. None of the four has been hit yet, and each of this extremely lucky, dumped litter finds a home. Ruth goes for unusual when she chooses Walter: long nose, pale lime eyes, all white except for a solid black tail and a large black spot falling casually over his back. Another unusual feature arrives later in life. Walter grows into a 16-pound hunk of sweetness, one of the most cooperative models in this book.

Back in civilization Ruth realizes the gregarious Walt needs a playmate. Looking at a litter of all-black kittens, her boyfriend claims the only girl of the four winked at her. Okay, she had to be "it." Ruby is her own cat. In the three hours I paint at Ruth's there is no interaction between the "play-mates." "Oh, well," Ruth says of the petite, aloof black cat, "I honor Ruby's independence and love of adventure by letting her come and go as she pleases. This is important to her."

Homebody Walt disappears. Ruth posts signs everywhere, runs ads in all the papers (most newspapers will run free ads for lost or found pets as a public service), and registers his description at the local shelter, should Walt show up.

Six months later the shelter phones her back-up number, that of her neighbor Patti. Patti rushes to the shelter but cannot identify the shadow of a cat that is supposedly Walter. Ruth does recognize him and months of fearing the worst end. The Durham Animal Shelter evidently cross-checks each animal that comes in with their lost-and-found report even six months after it has been

logged! So between excellent work on the shelter's part and kind strangers bringing him in, Walter is extremely lucky again, but...

Out on the road and out in the sun his left ear blisters and will not heal. The biopsy comes back as cancer. The ear is removed. Evidently skin cancer strikes animals too.

*Esmerelda*

ESMERELDA | The bus drops Debbie two blocks away from St. Francis Animal Hospital where she works. Always conscious of animals, one day Deb spies a cat crouched under a bush just yards away from heavy traffic. She reaches under and picks the large calico up. No resistance. She carries the calm cat to the clinic without a struggle. There, the veterinarian finds her in perfect health and spayed. Ads are placed, posters posted announcing, "Found cat." No calls or inquiries come forth, and the calico continues adapting to her surroundings.

My veterinarian, Margie Lindeke, gets tired of calling

the stray *Kitty-Kitty*. She hits on the name Esmerelda, which sticks immediately. Although Esmerelda initially is dying to go outside into heavy traffic, she becomes very comfortable lounging across Margie's desk or Linda's reception counter where she expertly surveys the clients, shares Debbie's snacks, explores every box delivered, both inside and out, and in general becomes one with the place. Talk of finding her a good home stops. She *is* home—at the vet's.

When I am commissioned to do an outside mural, 38'x18', at my vet's, her soul-mate dog, Pogo, is featured in the foreground and the pony from childhood, Intrepid, is seen from the window, along with Gomer, a Tennessee walker horse, who lived to be 33. Central to the image is Esmerelda, 5 x 8 feet, up on a sink, with a mischievous smile. I know that some day some person will drive by and look at that huge cat in this mural and say, "Dang, if that doesn't look like .....!"

*Esmerelda Amongst Clutter*

*Merlin*

MERLIN | Mimi and Daniel answer an ad giving away kittens. They choose solid white twin boys - one wiggly, the other placid. The calm Merlin is rendered exhausted by his hyper brother, Milo. Outside he is fine, but inside Milo rains down pure terror. The straw breaks when, climbing into his cat bed and looking directly into Mimi's eyes, he urinates. He is not happy. Mimi gets the message and phones his original people, who are happy to take the handsome neutered cat back as an outdoor cat.

Merlin does not miss his brother, but bonds closer to his human parents and dog Sadie. He rules a house and approximately six acres. New people move in next door with three male cats and install cat doors in their new home. Merlin's perfect world comes to an abrupt end. He tells the new cats to leave in every way he knows how, sometimes getting the worst of it.

Next, strangely enough, Milo, the hyper brother, and his family move in across the street. Merlin holds no sentimental feelings towards his brother, and as directly as possible asks him to leave, too. Merlin is now agitated, nervous, angry and torn up. His people are sad and anxious about his predicament and don't know what to do.

Then the neighbors with the cat doors evidently find Merlin in their house holding forth. Mimi and Daniel come to realize that to keep the peace Merlin has to remain exclusively indoors. And indeed, the neighbor-hood regains its tranquility, but a certain regal cat still yearns to go out. I mention that my Mr. Indoor/Outdoor, a.k.a. Roma, goes on daily walks with me, and it satis-

fies that need for him (plus, of course, his herbal remedies help.) Mimi and Daniel evidently listened to my ideas as the three now go on walks, Merlin adjusting to a harness and retractable leash.

*Sixty Feet Up*

SIXTY FEET UP | Avi, the Abyssinian, is once again up a tree, unable to get down. Four days sky-high and yowling piteously. Her throat is sore and her human, Lauren, is an emotional wreck. Lauren comes home early to meet up with the tree men cat-rescue team. Armed with cleats, rope and a pillowcase, one man goes straight up 60 feet or more. He asks, "Will she scratch me when I try to get her in the case?" Hell no, she won't. Avi knows the routine. She walks unassisted right into the opened pillowcase. She is lowered down purring as she heads to food, water, dry home and her relieved mom.

*Kevin with Cats*

FOUR CATS AND THEIR FELLOW | Last New Year's Eve my friends want to stay. I want to go, so I go up open stairs to a loft-like room where all the coats are lying across a bed. I camouflage myself amongst the coats and go half to sleep. A cat finding me snuggles into my arms. What is supposed to be a ten-minute nap turns into an hour. Party guests come and get their coats; some join us while the cat stays safe by my side under the coat.

When I make the list for this book, I include my New Year's Eve companion. Her person, Kevin, I only know from the party scene. At his house, now minus 70 people, he celebrates the end of tax season with calico Cindy

lounging across his raised, crooked arm as he dances around the room with a tall glass of champagne. She is the mother of Tuny and Potter, my bed friend. Kevin works at the university as an account- ant. Here, out on ten acres, he lives with four cats and a black-lab mix in the Tower House.

This crazy maze of a house is made for cats, with its breezeway, open fireplace, lofts and miles of circling deck. The rustic fireplace faces out into the kitchen, the backside makes up a wall in the bathroom beside the tub. Cats slip through rock tunnel- ways, popping their heads out to watch Kevin in the tub. Another wonderful cat feature in this timber-framed house is the perches. Several cats are high up on beams waiting for their person to go warm their bed.

It's now springtime. All the buds are popping, windows are open and there are plenty of beams to rest on; this crew is mostly mellow. I can't imagine any cat not loving life here.

*Bribing Winston*

**BRIBING WINSTON** | Of Terri's five cats, it is shy Winston she most wants to have included in this book project. He was her baby before she could have a human one. Winston is not "getting it," and portraying this cat in any fashion is not easily done. First we are on her bed with dry food; then under it with wet food; then the cat exits. We tiptoe from behind, following the elusive cat from room to room. For a few moments I paint Winston inhaling a can of freshly opened tuna. Quickly satiated, he runs down into the basement. Terri has to leave to pick up her son Alex. "Don't worry; you'll find him." I never do. The painting is only half done. What I do is find a photo to cheat from. All the other cats here are very friendly and, unlike Winston, in view.

*Mittens*

*Mooey the Magnificent*

MOOEY | Dad calls from NYC with this serious tone, unusually polite. Something is amiss, and I'm about to find out what. Would I take Mooey? My parents have had it. The rug cleaning bill has just surpassed the $1000.00 mark: Mooey's handiwork. They don't know where to turn.

Mooey was rescued about a decade ago by my brother. A 19-year-old girl he knew left town and forgot to leave out food for the cat. By Mooey's behavior, Jonathan suspects further abuse, but rather than investigate he simply takes her by Yellow Cab to his studio apartment. For several years she stays with him in his very small place. She grows fat and lethargic. Jon knows she will have a better quality of life with our folks, and she does, shedding 10 of her 20 pounds.

Thanksgiving I'm to bring her to North Carolina via plane. I'm not thrilled. The magic moment has arrived. The Moo yowls all the way to the airport. The nice man seated next to me talks of their cats and how he and his wife love them. Encouraged, I take Moo out of her cage. She pukes. Some lands on this guy. I apologize, but he becomes icy. Moo starts howling and this guy, cat lover though he claims to be, has his newspaper up like a barrier. The flight attendant tells him there are no other seats.

Here in North Carolina Mooey loves being outside in the fenced yard. She still has the occasional accident, but my floors are cement and clean-up is easy; besides, happily leaving apartment life far behind, this New York City cat spends most of her time outside.

PROMISE TO TWEETY | Richard Best comes to my attention as friends phone insisting I check out this feral cat activist that is all over the news. Apparently he and his girlfriend, Diane Thomas, have been charged with feeding a colony of feral cats too close to an upscale compound of condominiums. In the three years of their involvement, they've gotten 15 cats out of the area and have only two more to go.

The board members of the converted tobacco warehouses want the feeding stopped immediately. Mr. X. has been seen in the dead of winter snatching food pans up from kittens as they come to eat; his wife, Mrs. X., has plastered the hallways, elevator, and doors with posters of the dangerous activities of Richard and Diane; another condo dweller has had to be restrained as he attempts to attack feral cat activist Diane. In his rage he stomps on a humane trap until it is flattened. At this point I am wondering who should be suing who. The animal shelter suggests a small gate be installed in the fence and the two cats be fed on the other side. The board refuses this offer. Finally the lawyers and all involved settle on feeding the cats 100 feet off the property, much better than a $500.00 fine for each "feeding incident."

Until Richard and Diane's involvement with this colony of

*Hope, Faith and Floyd*

strays, they have had no prior relationships with cats. Diane simply asks security guard Bill Parrish about them. Bill is feeding the colony the four days he is on duty. Diane takes on the responsibility of feeding the crew the three days Bill is off. She notices they are not thriving, and in fact, several look very sick. The kittens are not making it through the winter. R & D contact animal welfare groups but they are not set up to take on this type of situation. Feral cat colonies fall between all the cracks.

   Over time R & D catch several cats in acutely compromised condition. "Despite the battered cats using litter boxes our place is a mess. We know nothing about cats." Veterinarian tests come out positive for FIV and FELV. Subsequently the cats fall further and die. R & D are desperate to make things better. They know there has to be a way.

Independent Animal Rescue suggests Operation Catnip, a Raleigh-based non-profit that for free, or next to it, spays/neuters, vaccinates and clips the ear of feral cats to be returned to their original environment. "Operation Catnip loans us five humane traps and we catch five cats that get the works. Next month, same deal: five cats get trapped/neutered/released. Known as TNR. All our females have been pregnant.

"The cat that got it all started for us we name Tweety," Diane says. "Tweety comes running to me; she waits for my car. She gives me air rubs, rolling and acting like she wants to get close, but just cannot. Then one day she rubs against me and climbs into my lap. She follows me to the door. Tweety figures out where we are on the second floor, climbs up on the shed like an acrobat, gets to our ledge, peers in and meows. We aren't cat people, we don't know anything, but this is breaking our hearts. We let her in. She plays with everything and anyone. Scooter, terrier-mix, loves her. She loves to sit on Rick's drafting table, stroke his face, and play with his pencil as he works. She wants to be close to us. She is diagnosed with feline leukemia and FIV. It is the worst of years and the best of years. The vets all love her, too. They bring in their own cats for her blood transfusions. When she dies, I make the promise to her that I will save as many cats as I can."

In the adoption room the adoptable ones scatter. Diane brings out food. Three-legged (steel-jaw trap) Hope is a tiny little food meister as she zips around inhaling every morsel. Diane explains, "You can't leave an automatic feeder out for cats that have known hunger. They don't know when to stop

*Promise to Tweety*

eating." And indeed, smoke-colored Hope acts insatiable around treats. One-eyed Faith is slower and shyer, and gray and white Floyd is tame enough to get within 18 inches of me. All the rescues eventually relax and at least become sociable with their immediate families. Diane has authored adoption forms. She knows all the questions to ask potential adoptees. It is just two years since *joie de vivre* Tweety has died, and already over 200 cats have been rescued from bleak existences. And to think I found these two people through a lawsuit posted against their altruism!

*Models Eating the Prop*

PASSIVE FATE—ACTIVE SEARCH | My imme-
diate neighbors, Kim and Barry, are awaiting their new
kitten, Mia. I am waiting with them when a familiar car
drives up. Hey! It's Diane Thomas. Diane found Mia in
the road next to a dead sibling. The kitten was at first terrified, Diane had to return with bait and a net. Success! The
little tabby is in a great permanent home, joining three
others.

Kim used to think she'd arrive by her cat family
members by fateful occurrences that would bring them
directly to her, but now, "Whether I do the rescuing or
someone else does the end result is the same. Someone gets
a home now."

On a rural Alabama highway, Max arrives in a fateful
way. Kim's mother witnesses as something living is hurled
from the pick-up truck in front
of her. She stops and finds a
dazed, bloody, scraped-up
kitten. This is how fate hands
Max to Kim.

On another fateful night a
few years before the Max inci-
dent, Kim finds Hope. Needing

*Zeke Waking Up*

to unwind, she spontaneously goes for a drive after work. Her headlights bounce off a small creature's eyes. She swerves, missing the kitten, hitting a pole that manages to rip off half her Dad's Buick bumper. Itsy-bitsy calico Hope beelines to her. At the vet's she collapses; she has used all the last of her energy to be saved. The following two cats show up in less dramatic ways. Kim now feels waiting passively for animals to show up doesn't help adequately.

She adopts Zeke, a runt from the Cat Hospital, freeing up their adoption cage so their good work can continue. Zeke wasn't homeless, but brought in by his first home to be euthanized along with his mother. He was a runt, and a toddler tripped over and fell on top of him. He was in the way. In his new home he fits right in, playing with Mia,

 groomed by Hope, and tolerated by Max. When cut flowers are brought over, this inside crew really chows down.

*Lola*

LOLA, IN HER NY LOFT | Back in New York, my folks tell me to check out the cat who resides with their friends Jamie and Bill. Bill is an artist, and they live in a huge Soho loft with bull's-eye tabby Lola. However, Dad warns, "She is beautiful, but you might never see her." Dad is right – almost. I see the cat, but she is terribly agitated.

Bill explains, "At the moment she is completely wired about the birds. If she had the chance she would be a major hunter." Pigeons are nesting outside one of the windows, causing Lola to pace back and forth, around and about, muttering and twitching her tail, focused to the core of her being on these birds. When not on bird patrol, Lola entertains herself by fishing things out of Jamie's chest of drawers – like an entire scarf collection – or running around the place dragging one of Jamie's antique sock monkeys. When Jamie abandons Lola by going on a business trip, the cat punishes her by taking objects belonging to her and scattering them about the loft.

Prior to the busy Lola, a calico named Kelly has reigned, having moved in without a hitch. After twelve years of living in the huge loft, she succumbs to kidney failure. When Bill returns to the vets for Kelly's empty carrier, the receptionist shows him the most beautiful kitten in the world, a tri-colored tabby – now, of course, known as Lola. Along with her mother and brother, she has been found in a lower Manhattan parking lot.

With the memory of how full-grown Kelly had adapted easily to her new home, Bill imagines it will be even easier for the new kitten. He is wrong. The small animal, overwhelmed in the huge space, vanishes. Jamie phones from work, "How is our new kitten?" Bill's voice shakes, as he hasn't a clue. In 3,600 square feet of loft, finding a place to hide is easy for Lola. For a full ten hours Bill pokes through stacks of paintings, bookshelves, closets, looking under, over and in every spot, and back again. He finally spies the little creature watching him from a snug place. Jamie comes home to meet the adorable cat, having completely missed the efforts of her panic-stricken husband. During the next few months, Lola continues to provide many hours of torment for her human parents by repeating her Houdini-like disappearance.

*Scarlett*

SCARLETT | An alleged crack house in an abandoned garage is up in flames. Possibly arson, probably a careless crackhead with a light. These details are moot points; what matters to the stray cat that lives there is getting her five kittens out alive. She makes five trips, each time returning to a structure that is further engulfed by flames and smoke. Every hair singed off her body, ears radically burned, eyes melting shut, she will not stop until she has rescued all five.

Firefighter David Giannelli finds the unconscious cat lying near her kittens. He carefully gathers the feline family up and goes directly to North Shore Animal Hospital's emergency room during the witching hours, when fires

claim most of their victims. Except for singed ears, the kittens look like they will make it. The young mother is less likely to. Word goes out around the world about this heroic cat. The masses pray for her, send cards with best wishes, and 7,000 offers to adopt her pour in. With deep burns lacing her skinny form, eyes still burned shut, named for her wounds, Scarlett hangs onto life. The world watches. The hospital is encouraged by her appetite.

After a month the white kitten succumbs to smoke inhalation. The litter is being hand-nursed and fed by hospital attendants. Scarlett is completely incapable of taking care of them. Deep burns can be insufferable, but somehow, through excellent medical care, treats and never-ending attention, in three months she is healed enough to go to a new home. A call goes out that only serious offers will be considered. Out of thousands of responses the final-ists are culled to ten. Karen Wellen's letter is written directly from the heart. She is interviewed by phone and in person, her home videoed for inspection. Karen mentions in the letter having gone through a terrible accident and surviving. She knows on a very deep level what Scarlett has been through. Her home is selected. Two pairs of kittens go to two top finalists. The media, along with the world, lie in wait for Scarlett's entry into her new digs.

In Milton Wellen's appliance store, rows of TVs tuned to every channel offer Scarlett's homecoming! Wife Rita, daughter Karen and Scarlett are there in the center of the buzz. Milton proudly announces to all that from their home in Brooklyn Scarlett will soon be moving to the West Village with his daughter, the writer. That is five years ago, and here I am visiting with the famous cat in Brooklyn. Scarlett never left.

Scarlett is now a solid 16 pounds, with a full, shiny calico coat. The deep scars on her legs and feet, near-hairless face, oddly upturned eyes and nubbed ears bear witness to her ordeal, and she receives eye lubricant three times a day. I find her to be a perfect model as she is accustomed to attention. Her 1932 townhouse is filled with three floors of art collections. Frank Sinatra's eight-foot model of the Empire State Building, acquired at auction, serves perfectly as a backdrop to this New York cat that owns the town. Mealtime is when she tells her humans that her food is out. Having been hungry early in life, she tends to be obsessive about food. Rita tries to moderate her calorie intake. To pose for me, though, she needs no bribing. She enjoys being surrounded by people.

Karen is leaving once more to give a talk to school kids. She is kept very busy between her own life and lecturing on Scarlett's story, leading into the subject of respect for all living creatures and good animal stewardship. Sometimes travel is paid for, or she is taken out for a meal, but primarily it is all done on her time and expense. She follows the Wellen family tradition of compassion. She recalls her mother Rita helping strays. At the appliance store her father and brother Bob feed a colony of cats.

Some might say, "All for a cat?" But Scarlett is a symbol of loyalty, heroism, and the best stuff life is made of. The outpouring of love shown towards this individual taps into the highest good in mankind and unleashes the spirit of compassion onto all aspects of life.

*Kittens at a Sidewalk Booth*

PURRFECT FIT | I am struck by how many pet stores in Manhattan have affiliations with animal welfare groups trying to place homeless animals. A Cause for Paws, City Critters, Purrfect Pals are just a few. My niece's friend Zoe was led to her cat siblings through such a group. Parents Michael and Elizabeth have stopped with her to look at the animals Purrfect Pals have up for adoption in front of the Pet Stop store on Columbus Avenue. Sharon Zolden asks if they'd consider two. Without hesitation Zoe's mom answers, "Absolutely, but it would be great if at least one could be a marmalade cat." The brother and sister team Sharon has in mind are both marmalades!

An employee from the Center of Animal Protection and Care has phoned Purrfect Pals with an unusual request. Would Sharon pick up two newborn, motherless kittens? They are going to be euthanized promptly, as the center does not have the staff to feed them around the clock. The two kittens become Sharon's personal project. The first month of their lives they go to work on Wall Street hidden in her bag. She stows them under her desk, bottle-feeding and grooming them when no one is looking. Sharon does her best to place all her fostered animals in excellent homes, but these two she has a special investment in.

Four-year-old Zoe, now eight, goes with her parents to meet the ginger tabbies at Sharon's home. Sharon visits and approves their apartment. After forms are filled out and adoption fees paid, Marigold and Shivers move to Zoe's. Zoe's mom Elizabeth is a writer who works from her home office, assuring the cats almost full-time company. For New York City they have a luxurious amount of space and plenty of pigeons to watch. Marigold often sits at the window where she has learned to chirp like a bird. Weekends and summers the family goes to their beach house on Long Island Sound, where the cats enjoy a screened-in porch and

*Marigold and Shivers*

a ladder leading to a loft.

Marigold explores my paint box and rips into the cat treats. She has no interest in them. Neither does her brother. Elizabeth explains that they are food snobs because they get a special diet delivered monthly from the Pet Stop which led them to the marmalade tabbies. Zoe has a skin allergy to cats, so once a month the cats are bathed with a special shampoo, enabling her to pick them up and cuddle them without fear of developing a rash or itch.

I leave, feeling Sharon would be happy with this home. But I also wonder how many times, giving of heart and soul, she has taken on such special cases, only to relinquish them so she could do it all over again.

*Tommy and Madeline*

TOMMY | My sister Rachel and her daughter
Madeline, my niece, live with Tommy in New York City,
up the street from our parents, Madeline's grandparents,
of course. The addition of a cat to their household is a real
surprise to me as I've always known Rachel to be a solid
dog person. Well, as big a surprise as it is to me, it is an
even bigger one for my niece.

Rachel places the new family member in her bathroom
to get acclimated. Our parents, as planned, collected their
grandchild from school, pretending it is just another day.
At the apartment Madeline is directed to go down the hall
and open the bathroom door very carefully. Four-year-old
Madeline is speechless. There, as if expecting her, sits
Tommy with his wise, adolescent kitten face. Maddie just

*Tommy with Teddy*

stares at first, then grins. She crouches down and ever so slowly approaches Tommy with great respect and gentleness. From then on the two are committed to each other.

A handsome orange and white tabby, Tommy plays with Madeline as if she were another cat. He hides, he pounces, she screams, he retreats. Then she hides, jumps out and chases him up the hall. When she captures him and hauls him around, he makes a really impressive armful because he is one large cat. Tommy sleeps on Maddie's bed at night along with her special doll, Molly, her three Shaggy bears, and often assorted other friends. In fact he sometimes sleeps on top of her. He wakes her at 6:45 a.m. sharp and awaits her return from school each day.

When Tommy's immediate family is out of town, he makes the 17-block trip south to his human grandparents. This transition is made without a hitch. I always know when he is at my folks' place because my mother will say, "You'll never guess who's here?" Very likely, of course, sleeping in Mom's laundry basket, the one with the freshly washed clothes. After Mooey, the cat they shipped 500 miles south to me, Tommy is viewed as a wonder cat; totally unlike the Moo, he uses a litter box and is reliably affectionate.

*Opal*

QUEEN OPAL | Opal is acting groggy. The vet says her blood sugar is down again so it's back on insulin. Late winter, 17 years ago, shelter volunteer, Susan Teer, returned my call looking to adopt a second cat. Little Zia was grieving the loss of tabby Tidy. Ms. Teer took the opportunity to snatch a cat from an inadequate foster home and drove directly to my house. The young tortie with opalescent eyes ignored Zia but Zia purred just happy to see another cat. Susan left saying, "This cat will always let her needs be known." How true, her mantra.

Opal tells me what time to wake up, when she doesn't like the food, when she needs more, and more, when the litter needs cleaning, outside, inside, outside, inside, pick me up, put me down. Being arthritic I cater to her requests for food to be brought to her or to be carried out to the garden or to the litter box or on the bed. Funny thing though, she manages to do all these things by herself when I'm not around.

At a potluck picnic held in my backyard years ago, I yell, "Make sure you don't let Opal out. At dusk she becomes a murderer." Sure enough, someone lets the demanding cat out, accusing me of exaggerating about her dusk hunting prowess. Well, are they shocked when she comes running over the picnic table with a large limp rodent, tail dragging through our food just minutes later. Man, right on cue.

Opal, though, does have her sweet, contemplative moments, too. Lying with Opal sitting sphinx-like on my chest, purring contently, eyes zoning out, a sweet gentle moment. Just us two. Tabby Zia comes zipping through and swats her on the butt, ending Opal's deep state of meditation and ending her moment of sole propriety over me. Opal is furious. She swings around and bats Zia around the ears. Zia is stunned that her minor indiscretion has caused such a fury. Opal will not even look in Zia's direction for three days.

Now Opal gets along with all cats and dogs. She presents herself to be groomed daily by the others. Oh, I have to go now. It is 5:57 p.m. and she is reminding me that dinner is at six.

*Gertie and Others*

GERTIE'S CAT HOSPITAL | Living with two geri-
atric cats with chronic disorders, I need a vet that is two
minutes away, so we make the big leap to the Cat Hospital.
Gertie, a long-haired Tabby, presides over the computer. At
one time she was a patient, but when her sister is killed by
dogs, Dr. Wendy Simpson is asked by the client to place
her. She realizes Gertie isn't safe where she lives but cannot
imagine her as strictly an indoor cat. At the Cat Hospital
she adapts very well to being inside; only once is she found
out, strolling up to the golf store.

Due to lymphocytic plasmacytic stomatitis – in short,
rotting teeth – all of Gertie's teeth have to be removed
except her canines. As she heals her friendly disposition

comes through. The doctor is hooked, thus landing the near toothless cat the role as goodwill ambassador for the clinic. She loves everyone: cats, people, and particularly men. If a man takes a seat in the reception area there is a good possibility she will snuggle into his lap. There are actually three resident cats: Oreo, brought in to be euthanized because she sheds, and Fluffy, who was going to be abandoned at a barn at age 17 because her person had died, but Gertie stands out, for she places herself wherever she will get the optimum amount of attention.

Dr. Simpson is allergic to most animals but not to the cats. With her asthma she has never gone to the ER due to cats or even had to use her inhaler. With other species she has had many close calls. She is truly connected to cats as a healer, and both my old girls are doing well with her concentrated efforts. And Opal's blood sugar is more easily monitored at Gertie's Hospital, only five minutes away in bad traffic.

*Mona Lisa and Baldasara*

MONA LISA AND CEDAR | As I cut through the Bisdee's backyard, through the sliding glass doors, Mona Lisa watches me with big round eyes. Visiting at her place, I see she thinks I'm okay and her humans, Michael and Sandy, are okay, but it is their son Cedar she loves. We have permission to pet her only on the head. Cedar can carry her around upside down, rub her belly, stroke her back, and growl at her, and she rolls over purring at him. If anyone else attempts any of the above, she will retaliate promptly. As Sandy Bisdee states, "I trust my snake Baldasara more than the cat." The cat is now at the snake's cage batting the glass furiously. "Stop that, Mona." She does.

Sandy, realizing her only child, nine-year-old Cedar, is genuinely lonely at times, asks a horse vet to find him a

kitten. The vet chooses one out of a litter of six and names her Mona Lisa. Young Cedar and the kitten bond instantly. Sandy now says of Mona, "We have an understanding. She likes my company, but when Cedar arrives she leaves me." Cedar, now 16 years old, is at his after-school job and not here to be interviewed. "Mona gives him the opportunity to love someone fully."

Coming home from the shelter with a litter of sickly kittens, I stop to show Cedar. With a smile that encompasses his whole face, eyes sparkling, he exudes, "Oh, they're so sweet; they're beautiful!" Mona Lisa has done a great job training a future cat advocate. Sandy did well recognizing how a pet would improve her son's life. And what a lucky Hillsborough, North Carolina, barn-born kitten!

*In the Playroom*

CONTINUUM | Back in 1983 I am contacted by a very sophisticated business woman, Deborah Kerpel, to do a portrait of her best friend Scruggs, a B&W cat. Ms. Kerpel, with her classic features, I feel, will be fun to paint, so I successfully talk her into getting a double portrait done. At the time I am pleased with the portrait, but my client is fussy. She takes me out to lunch to discuss changes she wants made. Seeing how ravenously I eat, she begins taking me out to lunch as a monthly routine.

I have met people that loved a pet, but up until this time I have never witnessed such a mutual bond. Scruggs sits high up in a pine tree waiting to spot her car approaching from several blocks away. Deb sees the B&W cat start shinnying down the trunk, leap onto the roof, then down to the A/C unit and greet her as she opens her car door. She awakes to find him under the covers with his head on the pillow next to her. He succumbs to leukemia three months before they come out with the shot for it. A year later the kittens she has adopted are darling, but the relationship with Scruggs was a once-in-a-lifetime deal.

Deb states, "Mattie is the most beautiful kitten ever born. The Elizabeth Taylor of cats." Now 16 years old Mattie never grooms her long tabby coat. She still sees clearly enough out of her big golden eyes to bring home a mouse. Toby, the young sprightly B&W male, we watch from the bay window as he leaps through the air doing a full flip after a bird. And another perfect somersault and another, fortunately never catching a thing.

Deb marries Don, becoming Mrs. Pausback. When they do not get pregnant they research adoption and eventually meet with success. Their son, Christian, nurtured like the adopted cats that came before him, is a talented athlete, calm and thoughtful. His three-year-old sister, Ava, cut from a completely different mold, tries to follow in her brother's footsteps. Both children love cats, but Ava adores dogs. Through her gregarious rambling, she asks me, "Do you have any adopted dogs? Cats? Children?" My dog died, cats of course I have, and children? Well, when I'm ready to adopt I'll be taking my friend Deb out to lunch for advice.

*Toby*

*Slim and Shadow*

AROUND THE CORNER | Hannah and I include the subdivision across the street in our weekly power walk. One day, alone, I take our normal route and, not distracted by chatting with Hannah, I notice more. One family has a cat flag on their mailbox. I ask the man gardening in the yard about it, explaining my current project. He calls the cats and his wife and goes looking for where the petite female Shadow is sleeping. Slim, primarily a black cat, has that iridescent fur that reflects purple and green highlights in the sun and a long Siamese face. Shadow also looks black but is really dark brown with a very sweet round face.

I'm delighted to find new subjects so close to home. Shadow comes from the Orange County Animal Shelter. Slim adopts Sharon and the gardener Alex by simply showing up all scrawny and hungry. Slim's new vet makes the discovery that he is already neutered, stating, "He probably did not enjoy the operation the first time around, so certainly let's not do it again."

One morning Slim is found outside dragging his leg. The X-ray shows the middle portion has been kicked to smithereens - a deer kick, most probably. A metal cage with screws is fitted onto the intact upper and lower portions of the limb. Astoundingly, the demolished bone reconstructs itself perfectly. No limp, no nothing, just a handsome, swarthy cat with an iridescent coat. I think, "That's it—the entire story of this peaceful home with the perfectly manicured yard." But Alex shows me a picture of the family property they are turning into a bed and break-fast. "Yes, it took a lot of work cleaning up after the over 100, maybe as many as 200, cats that passed through." Huh?!

In Murfreesboro, North Carolina, the word gets out that Alex's sister Helen is kind to cats. Locals dump unwanted cats and kittens at this large, turn-of-the-century home. Helen takes them in, gets all medical needs taken care of, organizes the rooms by colonies of cats with 10 or more to a room. At age 52 Helen marries for the first time a certain Dr. John. He neuters/spays every single member of the large household. Now age 74 with advanced Alzheimer's, Helen lives at home with around-the-clock care, by both humans and a cat.

Kentucky, the last of the cat clan, is with her 24/7, nuzzling and grooming her and purring by her side. I wonder who is taking care of the cats of Murfreesboro now?

*Sophie, Patrick and Puddencat*

SERENDIPITY | Across the dirt path from my place with its four felines is a home of three. When there is a meeting there, Patrick (Big Orange) is an expert at knowing who has no interest in fat cats. That's where he generally sits, right next to them, ignoring me and my pleas for His Magnificent's attention. Pudding cat (Little Orange) is a round-faced midget cat that skits around avoiding interaction with strangers. Both oranges have been adopted from the Orange County Animal Shelter.

Here is how Ms. Sophie comes into her family. Husband and wife team Mimi and Matt are in the chaotic process of building a hand-wrought timber-framed house, not seeking further distractions. Enroute to the building site, Mimi's car makes a large banging noise. She manages to get the car safely off the road and takes off on foot to the construction site. Mimi has walked two of the three

*Sophie and the Oranges*

miles when she spots in a ditch by the road two kittens, one dead, the other so weak it cannot make a sound. She places the frail animal inside her coat. At the vets the 15-ounce kitten is re-hydrated intravenously and the little leg is set. The vet makes no promises. It is touch and go for Sophie, but she survives. This is the only time I know of that a car busting an axle is a miracle, for where she had been found no car would normally have stopped and no one walked by.

Sophie loves her home with low windows, designed for cats. This is the only house I have ever been in where I wonder if the cats get rewarded for clawing the furniture. Actually, the cat-mauled furniture gives the new home a comfortable rustic look. Sophie adores Big Orange and instigates play with Little Orange. They act as though the sleek Sophie has been here since time began.

*Six out of Thirteen*

FARM SANCTUARY | Karin and I meet 14 years ago, just after she arrives from California with araucana hen Foozy and Bopsi Bunny. Then the stray cats Cubby and Tinky arrive. Chickens that have fallen off of trucks find refuge with Karin. At the Orange County Animal Shelter, swamped with rabbits a month after Easter, Karin adopts ten. Then she brings Sicilian donkey Pippin. Then smaller donkey Shady is found. When with fellow Feminists for Animal Rights she successfully bids on 4-H sheep. They then come to live with Karin. At a stock yard she finds a sickly little veal calf slated for slaughter. Today, Toubouli's back is over six feet high, and he weighs close to 2,000 pounds and will follow you anywhere for a rub on his massive head or a snack. Since his arrival, six more cows have missed their intended purpose and live here at the Farm Sanctuary.

Under a tree several mallard ducks rest with cats Toodie and Pugslee. The four mix-breed dogs greet us, but are pretty lazy and remain on the porch. George, a turkey strutting with full feathers up, joins us as we step around the rescued pot-belly pigs. Down the hill from Trip, Karin's partner, is Karin's two-bedroom trailer where nine cats co-exist peacefully. Originally there were 11 cats, but the two, Toodie and Pugslee, preferring to live with fewer of their species, walked up the road to Trip's and now reside there. At the trailer site a 30 x 30 foot bunny barn is being built. Karin is tempted to move in there and give the rabbits the trailer.

Things are on hold here at the Farm Sanctuary. Karin is pregnant with their second child. Taya is now three and a half and making funny faces. I realize she may possibly be imitating orange cat Boobie's scrunched in expression, but now she is mooing like a cow. Her first word is "Meow." The cats are too friendly. My paints are in jeopardy. Outside, in the cat-fenced area, I try to find more aloof subject matter. Kashi and Muesli, Siamese-mix siblings from the Chatham County pound, appear to be interested in paint too. What is with this crew? K & M are brought in with a litter of nine, but the facility will only keep three from each litter; six siblings are destroyed upon delivery.

The gray and white Sweet Kitty shows up at the Krishna Community and soon after gives birth to three. Through Karin and Trip's store, Earthwares, all three are adopted out while Sweet Kitty becomes an excellent store cat, greeting everyone. When the store closes she comes to the sanctuary. She gets along with everyone and seems to like paint, too.

I am happy that people like Karin exist and occasion-ally reproduce to carry on the good fight. Taya is learning to write. At her nursery school she posts pictures of animals with illegible messages to be kind to animals and not to eat them. I hope her generation is wiser and kinder than mine. People are the main problem with animals.

*Punkin and Baby Monster*

PUNKIN | Julie is not home, nor are any of the nine cats evident. The house is unlocked. Inside is feral Pearl behind the futon where she lives. The elderly brown tabby Effie is asleep on a chair. All others are well hidden. I call Julie at work. She is swamped and our appointment has slipped her mind. Wasn't I going to phone first? Probably. Anyway, I'm here so I go outside and find the orange-and-white tabby Pumpkin, who I'm told is the only friendly one. She is in fact a most cooperative model, sitting still in the sun, when out of nowhere a young fluffy blue-cream comes up and swats her on the backside. This is Baby Monster, the aloof beauty found with five others by Mama Dip's Restaurant.

Until ten years ago, Julie is exclusively a dog person. Returning one day to her apartment from doing laundry, a

pretty adolescent cat emerges from the sewer and follows her. She puts out milk for the youngster and goes to get more laundry. When she goes back out, the cat is gone and the milk is frozen over. Inside, out of the cold, she finds the young cat curled up in her warm fresh laundry. Julie is hooked, and Punkin is decidedly there to stay.

Julie's view of cats changes. She notices strays, forgotten cats. She sees that there is a great need to spay/neuter, to help end unnecessary suffering. She begins to take note and soon moves into action, trapping, altering, and managing to place most of them, all at her own expense and time. She has rescued over 200 felines. At her house live mostly unadoptable ferals and, of course, the seductress Punkin. Other animal welfare people have told me of her success in stabilizing whole areas of strays and of her plans to open a no-kill shelter.

Last spring Julie visits the largest no-kill shelter in the country, Utah's Best Friends Animal Sanctuary. She now has photos of all the buildings and has located a lot. Her husband Frank Cole, a builder of fine homes, will be building the state-of-the-art no-kill shelter. She will make it happen. The feral situation appears to be endless, and everyone needs to do something.

*The Queen Mother, Lucy*

IMPERFECT PERFECT | Feral cat activist Julie Smith tells me of Debbie Meyer, a newspaper columnist who writes informative articles on animals. We finally meet at her serene home on a pond. I sense this is going to be good.

Three friendly horses approach me and walk right by to Debbie with the hay. In the barn, tabby Violet peers down. Orange tabby Dante inspects my car. Dogs Zelda and Buzz are leaping up in their pen to be noticed. Betsy, the adopted potbelly pig, is not in view. Inside this airy house a one-eyed B&W cat, Schroedinger, greets us, and three-legged black cat Ella scoots by. The youngest cat, Steward, bounds up the stairs, challenging Debbie to race. When they return, Steward jumps up on the table introducing herself to me. One eye is gone, the other milky. "Hey, this cat is blind." Conjunctivitis as a kitten has taken most of her sight. She can see a little out of the overcast eye, Debbie claims, but I think she is just extremely adapted to this house.

At animal shelters I have seen people surrender animals to face uncertain futures because they are moving, the animal sheds, or it doesn't match the new couch; the list of heartless reasons goes on. At Debbie and Eric's exquisite new home, the philosophy is the opposite. "You can't replace a life, but you can a couch." Actually, she's talking about the dog Buzz destroying the same couch – twice!

Debbie has written on homeopathy for animals, feral cat colonies, good horse care, and a woman that tamed a cat by reading to her nightly from the Bible. An irate reader writes to accuse her of "just" caring about animals. As it turns out, Debbie chairs a mentoring program for youths, works full-time at Duke on one of the world's most important scientific weeklies, and facilitates a column at the Chapel Hill newspaper called *My View*. Ordinary people get to write on a subject near and dear to them. Would the complainer take in blind amputee cats or care enough about people to help them be heard?

Eric comes home and one-eyed Schroedinger gets into his lap; allergic Eric takes Beclovent to make this relation-ship possible. Blind Steward reaches out to me with a soft paw. She wants a belly rub. The Queen Mother, cat Lucy, with one blue eye, the other yellow, nearing 20 years, looks out over the pond. Rumor sits up high on an archi-tectural feature surveying us. Ella shakes her head to the right for Debbie to scratch under her chin. With her right leg missing, she can't reach that spot. "Part of the big attraction in getting involved with animals is that they easily make us feel like heroes. Hands-on feels better than giving $1000.00. I do something as simple as loan a trap. A cat gets caught and spayed and many lives don't suffer in vain." Nobody is suffering at this location.

*Indigo and Cleo*

SISTERHOOD | As I am driving to a job interview, a scrawny kitten leaps out. I am late so I take the scraggly creature along. She climbs all over my two male interviewers who do not act the least bit charmed. I phone to see if I have been hired. The two dullards think I am a flake. "Oh, would it have been better if I had squashed the kitten? Doesn't this job take quick thinking and caring?" I get the job.

Returning from the interview, I realize this weak little kitten will have a rough time at my place so I stop at Dede's. She picks the runny-eyed one up and exclaims, "I'll keep her." I am shocked. Easiest placement ever. "I knew the moment you brought her to me. I've placed many strays, but never felt such an immediate heart connection. It feels like my beloved cat Zephyr is back."

Eleven years ago Dede liberates blue-cream tabby sisters Indigo and Eden from the Durham Animal Shelter. She had planned to get only the healthier of the two, but Indigo would not go without her sister Eden. Dede relents and falls into the role of protecting the weaker kitten. "Eden was my fragile little egg." Six years later the hefty sisters are welcoming towards the new member of their family, brown-tabby Cleo. Indigo particularly takes her under her wing (paw). The three sleep, tussle, play, and groom each other all very harmoniously. When Cleo goes into heat and starts howl-

*Eden's Scratching Couch*

ing, Eden switches. Cleo climbs in between her two feline companions and is attacked unmercifully by Eden. Blood is everywhere. Dede rushes Cleo to the emergency clinic. Nothing, it seems, will ever be the same again. "Eden has gone from being my fragile little egg to being a hard-boiled egg."

During the day the cats are separated; at night Dede's bed is the peace zone where all four sleep unchallenged. Dede moves with the three spayed cats to a smaller house in the country, where no one can be separated. Together they go for walks, and Dede notices they are getting along once again. The following move really makes things go back to normal, but sometimes Cleo just can't help herself. She will pounce all over the two matrons, inciting them to chase her; she then runs and leaps into Dede's lap, purring loudly and wiggling in a laughing manner: "Ha! You can't get me. I'm the Baby!" The old egg, Eden, still sees herself as the cuddly little baby. Indigo is a wise old soul that remains steadfast in her overseeing of this household with its two eternal babies!

*Earle and Budakon*

EARLE AND BUDAKON | Bonnie is having empty-nest syndrome with her son off to college. "I want to have another baby. Egads! What am I saying? I better adopt a kitten, fast." She does promptly. From the shelter she brings home a fluff ball, naming him Earle. He stretches out and rolls on his back in a most enticing way, then bounces away. By the next week Baby Earle has doubled in size.

When I next see the massive cat with cocked head, he is sprawled on his back and resembles a 20-pound bear rug. "Oh, how huggable." "Not really, he will bite you if you touch him. He is just for looking." To be so gorgeous and so aloof! "Bonnie, there is a cat in your backyard and another lying on your front-door mat. Aren't they terrified of him? If he sat on them he'd squash them!" "No, they know he can't be bothered. His size keeps him secure; he goes right by them."

Steve and Bonnie are slowly starting to live together. To see how the cats will do in their combined household, first petite princess cat, Budakon, all of five pounds, is moved in. For the first time ever, Earle directs his snarl at another cat. She is unfazed and ignores him. In time, he mostly ignores her. She has a huge voice with a huge need for attention. In contrast over-sized Earle has a peep of a voice and prefers no physical contact. Despite Budakon's previous person having her declawed, the cat can be a ferocious hunter. Easter Sunday she lunges onto a squirrel, wrapping her clawless paws around the frightened animal's neck as it runs, finally breaking its neck. She very proudly drags the dead squirrel, almost equal to her size, up the porch stairs. Soon after she isn't so lucky. Steve finds her outside, half dead, with her neck slit. Nursing her back to health, he realizes that without front claws the great outdoors is a lopsided gamble not to be risked. Both cats are now indoors, but Budakon goes out on the roof peering down like a gargoyle. Inside she stays clear of the hissy giant and commands the attention of her loving parents.

*Thomas*

THOMAS EUGENE O'REILLY III | I'm in West Virginia for the first time. I have a TV interview and a book signing, but the main mission is to do monoprints of Max, my agent Patrick's cat companion. His PR manager, Amanda, generously offers me a place to stay, and Patrick mentions that I might include Thomas, the cat she lives with. Well, here it is 7:10 a.m., and I'm looking at this hefty blue-cream tabby, and he is looking at me. I say to Thomas, "What do I tell the world about you?" "That I am a most wonderful guy, above and beyond all cats, and that you love me very much. Hey, do you have any treats for me?" No, I don't. Exit Thomas.

When Amanda is first on her own, moving out from her folks' house, with its continually growing population of cats, one of her top priorities is to find a cat to adopt.

*I Can't Help Myself*

She'd never lived without one. Her family home, located on a rural West Virginia road, is a prime spot for throw-away animals. Most of these animals end up finding their way to what friends have nick-named the Unofficial Boone County Animal Refuge.

Amanda gets Thomas from a friend who knows a friend whose cat has had kittens. A couple of years later, she brings home a new kitten – born from a stray dropped at her parents – whom Thomas enjoys immensely, but then he grows bored with her as she gets older. Soon after Amanda and her cat-kids move back into her folks' house, but now she and Thomas are on their own again while he helps her through graduate school. The other cat is more suited to remain in the country where she can roam freely and be groomed by her mother cat.

During his stay there and on visits, the handsome Thomas gets along with the twelve cats at his human grandparents', primarily because he ignores them. The two younger cats he plays with occasionally. His attitude appears to be, "I like kittens; I dislike cats." There are many humans who feel that way, too. What I tell them and Thomas is this: "If you give a cat a chance, you'll have a good friend." Not that humans, and certainly not cats, ever listen to me.

*Max*

MAXIMILLIAN GREYSTONE III | Paula and Patrick are not cat people when Max adopts them. On a walk down a country road in Lavalette, West Virginia, they spy a small gray animal getting off a stoop and sauntering down a long driveway toward them. Given the distance P&P cannot tell if it is a cat or a dog. They wait and walking up to them is this very friendly young cat with spring green eyes. He joins them for quite a ways until a dog challenges him. Paula shields the little cat. Patrick chases the dog away. Back at the place where they found him, the woman who answers the door says, "No, he's not my cat, he just showed up." Her Sheltie has not been welcoming; this is not a permanent home. "Why don't you keep him?" So Paula says to Patrick, "Let's see if he follows us all the way home; no coaxing." It's a quarter mile walk, but he does, and P&P, though not cat people, decide that at least temporarily the little stray can stay on the screened porch.

Paula comes home from the office the next day with the works, collar, litter box, food bowl, etc., only to find that the cat is GONE! – escaped off the porch through a hole in the screen. P&P search everywhere, not knowing where to start. Three days later the cat turns up on a neighbor's deck. P&P are shocked by how delighted they are to have him back, and argue over a name. Patrick wants "Greystone" and Paula wants "Max." The compromise is to call him Maximillian Greystone III, but "Max" for short.

While P&P learn more about cats, Max becomes more like a dog; he is sloppy with his food, drags his dishes around the floor, waits for the mailman, wags his tail like a puppy and takes up boxing. Yes, boxing. Patrick somehow gets it all started, but the cat comes up with his own rules. Max can really deliver a good left-right combination. As Patrick says, "He is fascinated by boxing and is quite good at it." I witness as Max starts a match by staring Patrick in the eye, then punching (not clawing, mind you) his hand. The match is on with a fury as the two bop each other and shield against each other's blows. It ends when Max decides it is over and scampers off.

Maximillian Greystone III is now a full-time indoor cat. Out on the screened-in porch his tail twitches and he mutters curse words as a B&W cat traverses his property. Embedded in his rear leg is a bb the vet detected. With stray dogs, cars, idiots with guns, any number of things can happen. Max stays in, charging up the house with his energy. He zooms around like a kitten. As do his folks, Max likes dogs, so at some point they hope a compatible one will join the family.

*Regis and Ginger*

REGIS | Patrick asks his vets Dr. Ball and Dr. Staley if they know of any spectacular cat stories. Regis, a cat named after the famous game-show host, has recently been placed through her clinic. Like his namesake, the cat can really hold his own in conversation. I agree that a talking cat is intriguing enough to investigate. Paula offers to transport me to meet Regis.

In the small town of Kenova, we find the house easily as a flame-point Siamese is waiting for us outside the front door. This is Ginger. Inside we meet Beth and her children, Brittany, Cassidy and Regis, a solid white cat with bright, orange-striped tail and a couple of small, orange markings. This is how Regis gets found. Sandy, an employee at the Huntington Dog and Cat Hospital, notices one day that the cats at her home are making a commotion. There sits this stray cat chatting away. Sandy takes him to work with her, where he continues the conversation. At the clinic he entertains everyone with his continual chatter. Veterinarian assistant Beth Parsons says she'll take him home and try him out with her cats.

Here at Beth's we are sitting on the floor. Regis is loung-ing on Paula. For a cat that has only been here a month, he is completely at home and quiet. Ginger comes in and gives me a soft meow. I look at Regis and say, "Okay, that's your cue." Nothing. His eyes won't leave Ginger. He desperately wants her to accept him. She is beginning to as they touch noses. There is a third cat, Olivia, that is too shy to make an appearance. When Regis gets too gregarious towards shy Olivia, Ginger will defend her. Regis respects Ginger's authority. He wants so badly to be friends with her. He still has not said a word, but he is very sweet.

The cats have all had tendonectomies, which is a procedure of cutting the last digital tendon, prohibiting a cat from putting their claws out. With this procedure nails have to be clipped scrupulously. In this case a corner of the upstairs carpet has come under attack, and to keep the peace with her partner, Beth has to take quick action and do something radical. This operation is less invasive and requires less recovery time than declawing. Like me, Beth prefers squirt bottles, scratching posts and training and leaving a cat with its full defenses. Two out of the three cat stories I've covered here in West Virginia involve cats that have been shot with a BB gun. No surprise, then, that all three cats are exclusively indoors! Regis is sitting inside my paint box, sniffing and investigating silently. We leave, having heard only the faintest peep. I think he used his voice to get his legendary name and a good secure home. At this point the laid-back Regis simply can't be bothered speaking for the sake of a visitor.

*Regis*

*Wild Boy*

SOUL MATES | At the General Store Cafe, Doug
Lorie points out his three cat-kids on the pet photo wall.
Doug is the chef, and he is just getting off from a long
shift. I follow him back to his place along some pretty
country roads. He lives down a dirt road that leads to a
long, serpentine drive curving up to the hand-built cabin
sitting on a hill. Down and up the path is a terraced
garden with goldfish pond and statuary.

Out on the deck, a large outside room, Doug reclines,
and Wild Boy, a B&W long, thick-coated cat with big
plush paws, plops down beside him in an identical posi-
tion. Some time ago, he and his former wife, Trish, fly
Annie, Spanky, Twiggy and Goose out to New Mexico
where Trish enrolls in acupuncture college and Doug
undertakes to teach high-school English. Here, in the high
desert country north of Santa Fe, there is no shortage of
dogs. Their neighbor, Edie, called by many The Dog Lady

of Chimayo, has eighty rescued canines secured in pens outside her house. The security promised by these pens is not complete, as the events that unfold will show. The other neighbor's dogs are given free range amongst the strays and marauding packs. Annie, an elderly tortie, gets the picture and never ventures outside. (She is now over 20 years old, possibly as old as 25.) This cat clan of four is used to having full range. They have had the good life of cat doors, gardens, decks, and streams. To bound them in is against everything. Then Twiggy is killed by a dog. For the sake of the entire family his body lies in state for a day, surrounded by flowers, incense and candles. Maybe Spanky and Goose will understand what happened and tread more carefully during their walks among the juniper and piñon.

Doug and Trish start feeding a feral cat through a ripped screen. Although wary, the cat shows up with regularity. Eventually Doug puts the food on the inside of the screen. When the cat tames a little, boom, Doug gets him to the vet. Releasing him back home, the now-dubbed Wild Boy starts making the venture inside to comfortable furniture and security, but still continues to go out. Doug visualizes being home in North Carolina with Wild Boy beside him safely in his garden. This vision becomes a daily meditation.

Goose, a magnificent Siamese, is then suddenly killed by a rescued Irish Wolf Hound. Circumstances take their toll. Trish chooses to stay in New Mexico. Doug flees back to North Carolina, flying the two survivors, Annie and Spanky, and of course Wild Boy, to the Pittsboro homestead. His meditation has become reality: hiking in the woods with Wild Boy, relaxing in the garden together, hanging out on the deck. Annie sleeps a lot these days, and Spanky stays close to companion Yvonne, who often works from home. Doug is downloading his e-mail. Wild Boy next to him spreads out across the printer. Doug goes to run his bath water extra high so WB, sitting on the ledge, can easily take a long drink. Doug says to me, "I'm in love with this cat." He then bends down and kisses the head of this New Mexican renegade, saying, "I'm in love with The Wildboy!" Wild Boy smiles at him. Yeah, he knows.

*Maximum Paws and Zip*

MAXIMUM PAWS AND ZIP | Someone tells me about seeing two of the most beautiful cats at the Dovecote Store out at Fearrington Village. I drive out there with every intention of featuring them, but what I really want are bookstore cats. As it turns out, in the same complex McIntyre's Fine Books also has two felines in residence. Although Dovecote's Simon and Merlin are indeed very beautiful, time and space are rapidly becoming scarce for this project. The staff at McIntyre's is pleased with my decision and feels the literary cats are most suitable to grace the pages of a book on cats.

B&W Zip grooms her hulking son as if he were a tiny kitten. They sleep curled up in each other's arms.

Maximum Paws is polydactyl, with two extra fingers on each paw. Bookseller Martha preferred naming him Thumbs Hemingway after all the multi-toed cats living on the Hemingway complex. I follow the cat trying to figure out the best angle to capture his broad feet. He leads me into an office, enjoys being petted, and then is on the move again. Up the stairs he sits still at last. Having given himself a partial bath, he leaps back downstairs, and I follow, into the children's section and then on to travel. Some paper crumples at the cash register, cueing him to run in that direction. Someone opens the front door, and so back up the stairs we go. Three hours of following Maximum around, and finally I have something resembling him. If this is his way of sabotaging me to prevent my having time to paint the Dovecote cats, it has worked.

Maximum and mom Zip have their jobs at the bookstore. They help with gift wrapping by playing with the ribbon. Maximum helps Peter check in books, particularly the paperwork. Zip keeps Robert company when he is at the computer. She also warms the laps of men with facial hair, as she is partial to them. Maximum protects his toys from imaginary thieves with a growl, but is most affable during book readings where he works hard to steal the show. If I give a talk here at McIntyre's, I certainly hope Maximum and Zip will make an appearance.

*Kittens*

ORPHANS | A litter of kittens needs a temporary home. I poll my co-housing neighborhood to see if anyone can take on the fun project of fostering a mother cat with kittens. Several kind people promise to help, but no one feels they can go beyond that. I know I can't. I'm maxed out with deadlines. A local teenager comes to me and requests I reconsider being a foster home myself. She will be there to help. So I call Independent Animal Rescue, founded by Leslie Mann. I set up my largest bathroom to accommodate a family.

Julie of IAR directs me to an orphaned litter at the Durham Animal Shelter. Before even meeting them, I name them Uno, Dos, Tres and Cuarto. The shelter is packed, three rooms of magnificent cats, floor to ceiling. The kittens are in isolation. They have been found motherless and starving. Looks like they still are, and Cuarto has died.

By evening residents line up to oooh and ahhh over Uno, Dos, Tres, now home in my bathroom. Mimi helps bathe them. Both Uno and Dos are calico tabbies with long scrawny faces, matching their scrawny bodies. Tres is a Siamese tabby with a flat round face. Despite early hardships, he has a roly-poly body and a continuous loud purr.

Next morning they scream at me like a nest of hungry birds. Runny poop is everywhere. Clean-up of kittens and area takes an hour. I am overwhelmed and I need to get other things done. Neighbor Maggie comes over for the next shift and renames them Lacy, Garbo and Bandit. I do the next two shifts and thank the Great Goddess when Maggie shows up again. The next two days are identical: eat, poop, sleep, poop, poop. Besides Maggie, the only neighbor to show up is the teenager, once, and this is to play with the presently clean kittens. When she leaves there is poop everywhere. I want to scream. So far the two girls are lethargic and not gaining any weight. Bandit is thriving.

After the second dose of medicine Garbo becomes spunky – climbing, biting her brother, demanding lots of attention. Lacy does nothing, sits, sleeps, falls over. We give her kitten milk through a dropper. I enlist ten-year-old Alli to hold her. She does this for an hour, and Lacy revives a little. Without a mother cat this is a huge job. Lacy is getting weaker. I phone medical professional Helen Cook who races over with an IV bag. We go upstairs to find Lacy has just died. The little female just lies there, limp. Maggie sounds strong when I tell her via phone, but isn't when she gets here. We tell Alli, who has bonded with Lacy. At her makeshift funeral, we encircle the small body, holding hands. Maggie sees the little orphan with her mother and brother free and happy on the other side. This helps, and we go to tend to the living.

The next day the two

*Lacy*

survivors seem to have grown overnight – all poop is in the litter box, all food is gone. Bandit leaps out of the tub and into my lap, wanting a tummy rub and chin scratch. Garbo is giving herself a full bath. The kids have turned the corner. Monday their photos get posted on the Internet; Tuesday they go to the vet's, and I get their adoption forms and contracts; Thursday they star in a cable access show; Sunday is their kitten shower; then they go to their new, permanent home. As Maggie says, these are the lucky ones. Had they not been found and taken to the shelter, they would have starved or become hawk food. Now they will be the center of someone's household.

*Bandit and Garbo*

## LOW COST NEUTER/SPAY PROGRAMS

For low cost spay/neuter programs in your area please call:

**SPAY/USA**

1-800-248-SPAY (7729)

## EDUCATION

A magazine dedicated to making this a more compassionate world for animals:

*The Animals Agenda*

3500 Boston Street, Suite 325

P.O.Box 25881

Baltimore, MD 21224

The largest no-kill animal shelter in America. They offer information on how to set-up a similar program in your area. This is also a great place to take a volunteer-work vacation.

**Best Friends Animal Sanctuary**

5001 Angel Canyon Drive

Kanab, Utah 84741-5000

Tel: 435-644-2001

## FERAL CATS

National organization that offers information and support for feral cat colonies. They publish a helpful newsletter, *Feral Cat Activist.*

**Alley Cat Allies**

1801 Belmont Road NW, Suite 201

Washington, DC 20009

Tel: 202-667-3630

www.alleycat.org

Organization that does neutering and spaying of feral cats for a small donation:

**Operation Catnip**

P.O.Box 90744, Raleigh, NC 27675

Tel: 919-779-7247

www.operationcatnip.org

Operation Catnip in Gainesville:
P.O. Box 141023, Gainesville, FL 32614-1023
(352) 380-0940
www.operationcatnip.com

Operation Catnip in Richmond:
P.O. Box 15522 Richmond, VA 23227
804-674-0660

The company that invented the humane trap 80 years ago and
will not manufacture or sell the crippling leghold trap:
**Tomahawk Live Trap**
P.O. Box 323
Tomahawk, WI 54487
Tel: 800-272-8727

## PRODUCTS I HAVE FOUND INVALUABLE
Before you or anyone you know gives up on an animal, please
try the remedy Abandonment & Abuse. It expedites the recov-
ery of animals acting out due to fear or trauma of any kind.
Flower essences for the health and emotional well being of
animals:
**Green Hope Farm**
P.O. Box 125
Meriden, NH  03770
Tel: 603-469-3662

If you live with a cat like my darling Roma you will want to
check into this biodegradable pet stain, odor and pheromone
extractor and stink finder light. I found these products in:
**Jeffers Pet Catalog**
P.O.Box 100
Dothan, AL 36302-0100
Tel: 800-533-3377

Health food for animals:
**Wysong** *"The Thinking Person's Pet Food"*
Wysong Corporation
1880 N. Eastman Road
Midland, MI 48642
www.wysong.net

Cat Book

Cat Fence-In does exactly that. It attaches to the top of fences and keeps cats from escaping.
**Cat Fence-In**
P.O.Box 795
Sparks, NV 89432
Tel: (888) 738-9099
www.catfencein.com

## ALTERNATIVE ANIMAL CARE

My homeopathic vet (the story *Caracals*) offers both less invasive treatments along with support to more mainstream methods. He works exclusively through phone consultations.
**Charles Loops, CVM**
38 Waddell Hollow Road
Pittsboro, NC 27312
Tel: 919-542-0442

Anita is a Reiki practitioner for animals, the art of healing touch. She works with her subjects both in person and via phone. Her story in *Cat Book* is *Healing Touch*.
**Anita Anglin**
P.O.Box 1294
Pittsboro, NC 27312
Tel: 919-545-2390

Healing touch for animals workshops:
**Komitor Healing Method, Inc.**
P.O.Box 262171
Highlands Ranch, CO 80163-2171
Tel: 303-470-6572
www.healingtouchforanimals.com

The story *Maia and Tuli Bear* is about animal communicator Tera Thomas's household. She does phone consultations.
**Hummingbird Farm**
P.O.Box 1603
Pittsboro, NC 27312
Tel: 919-545-0686

EMILY EVE WEINSTEIN, a native New Yorker, has studied art in France, England, and Virginia. The author-artist of *Moon Book* (1999), she has turned here to her lifelong fascination for cats, using the medium of monoprints. Ms. Weinstein, who does murals, portraiture and fine art, lives in Durham, North Carolina with cats Opal, Sophia, Casey and Roma.